ESCAPE FROM TERROR

ESCAPE FROM TERROR

Bill Basansky
with
David Manuel

Logos International   Plainfield, New Jersey

ESCAPE FROM TERROR
Copyright © 1976 by Logos International
All Rights Reserved
Printed in the United States of America
International Standard Book Number: 0-88270-158-4 (hardcover)
0-88270-159-2 (softcover)
0-88270-254-8 (pocket)
Library of Congress Catalog Card Number: 76-2327
Logos International, Plainfield, New Jersey 07061

Author's Note and Acknowledgments

Most of the events in this book took place during World War II, when I was a boy. I have told them, as fully as I could and to the best of my recollection, to my friend and collaborator, David, who then, by God's grace and guidance, brought them to life. After which, I did my best to make sure that they remained as faithful as possible to the spirit of what happened and the relationships involved. I have purposely avoided mentioning the name of our village in the Ukraine, to protect those who might still be living in its vicinity, and I have changed the names of those who might be embarrassed by the roles they played.

I would like to take this opportunity to thank the nation of America and its people for giving me a new home; my former Chancellor, Oral Roberts, for his faith and inspiration; Demos Shakarian, for his help and encouragement; and above all, my parents, brothers and sister for their love and support.

Bill Basansky

Co-author's Note

When I first heard Bill Basansky speak, as much as I was drawn by his spontaneous enthusiasm for Jesus Christ, when he went on to extol the virtues of America, I was put off by his seeming blindness to all that was wrong in our country, and his presentation of Communism as diabolically evil.

But then I got to know Bill, and to know his story. And at the same time, I read Aleksandr Solzhenitsyn's *The Gulag Archipelago,* which gave Bill Basanky's story meticulous documentation: Six million Ukrainians deliberately starved to death by the Communists in 1932 and 1933; 1.5 million Slavs forcibly repatriated from Germany and Eastern Europe at the end of World War II—and executed or imprisoned (*U.S. News and World Report,* July 14, 1975); 66 million deaths occurred in Russia's Destructive-Labor Camps as of 1959; 15 million prisoners in them right now (*Newsweek,* November 3, 1975). The mind loses its capacity to react to such figures.

Bill's story brought it all home, to the degree that I am now more grateful than I ever imagined I would be, to have been born and grown up in a country so free of fear. I am grateful, too, for the men God had first led here in the beginning and for new Americans like Bill, who know the sweetness of the liberty we take so much for granted.

David Manuel

List of Maps and Illustrations

The Ukraine was a seething cauldron in the winter of 1943. The once-vaunted German war machine was in full retreat all along the southern front. Yet they were determined to take the entire civilian population with them—for slave labor to free more Germans to fight in what all but the most fanatic recognized as a losing battle. Whole villages were being herded into convoys and forced to trek across the snowbound steppes, towards the cattlecars awaiting them in Romania. In one such village on the Dnieper River lived a family named Basansky—Ivan and Maria, their sons Alexei and Vasili, and daughter Lida, and Maria's grandmother, Babunia.

As dreadful as the Communist and then German occupations of the Ukraine had been, what now lay before the Basanskys, as they fled before the advancing Red Army, was an ordeal of nightmare proportions. For the Russians were taking no prisoners, soldiers or civilians, and those who had not already succumbed to starvation or the $-40°$ cold, were being indiscriminately slaughtered.

Only one thing sustained the Basanskys when all those around them were perishing: the indomitable faith of Babunia.

PART ONE

one

Across the river, a lone, white birch, shining in the noonday sun, stood out against the deep forest that stretched along the east bank as far as the eye could see. In front of us, the wide Dnieper flowed south toward the Black Sea, its smooth surface gleaming in the sunlight like white-silver armor. The air was perfectly still—not a leaf stirred in the wild pear tree in which the three of us crouched, as far up as we could get.

This strange peace—as if time itself were holding its breath—extended to the left of us as well, into our village on the edge of the Ukrainian steppes. The little mud-brick, thatched-roof houses nestled silently on either side of the dirt road, and there was no movement anywhere. True, the workers had gone into the wheat fields before dawn, but there should have been something—an old woman fetching water from the well in a two-bucket yoke, little children playing in the road, a grandfather smoking a home-rolled *makhorka* cigarette on his front stoop. It was as if the village were under a spell. . . .

Frowning, I glanced at my brother Alexei, who was scanning the trees on the opposite bank. At ten, he had a year's advantage over me and Georgi, our friend from school, and was thus our acknowledged leader. It was his idea that we take up this observation post (and try our own home-made "cigarettes"), and we readily agreed. War games had always been our favorite, and now, with the rush of events of that summer of 1941, and especially of the past few days as the reality of it all descended on our village, the games were, in a sense, no longer games.

"They've got to be in there somewhere," Alexei whispered, though there was no one within earshot for a kilometer in any direction. "You can't hide the whole Red Army!"

It seemed to me that they were doing a pretty good job of it, but I held my tongue and by sheer will tried to force my gaze into the screen of green foliage. Suddenly, about 200 meters upstream from the white birch, I thought I saw something move. It may have been a shifting shadow, but to me it was a turret swiveling.

"I see a T-34!" I half-shouted, referring to the newest tank the Russians had.

"Durak!" my brother hissed, "Dumb-head, you know what they had with them when they pulled out of the village: nothing bigger than some old *Pushkas*—anti-tank guns, and most of them horse-drawn." He shook his head, disgusted with me. "The heavy armor is up north, in front of Moscow and Kiev." And having thus dispensed with his woefully incompetent subordinate, he returned his attention to the far bank. And peace returned to our tree.

It was a magnificent tree, massive around the trunk but with large limbs low enough to be just right for climbing, and others far enough up so that you could really get some height. Standing atop the high, steep bank that rose almost like a cliff on our side of the river, it afforded an unparalleled view of the surrounding countryside. But what made it even more ideal as an observation post, as Alexei was quick to point out, was that in addition to being a good distance from the village, it was directly over a small creek that ran into the Dnieper. This creek, in turn, was joined by a dry gully that ran up behind the village, which meant that we could sneak to and from the village without being seen. Far below us lay our dog *Moryak,* "Sailor," patiently guarding our flanks and rear—and snapping at the occasional fly that threatened his own. I smiled and wished it were the end of September, instead of the middle of August, so that we could eat the pears that were just beginning to ripen around us.

"What if they start shooting?" Georgi ventured, beginning to realize for the first time this was not another one of Alexei's imaginary exercises. From what we had overheard the grown-ups say, and from the haste of the Russians' recent exit, it was apparent that the Germans were advancing eastward faster than expected and would probably reach the Dnieper within the next forty-eight hours.

Faster than expected—it seemed like the Germans were always advancing faster than expected, ever since Hitler had broken his non-aggression pact with Stalin on June 22, and given the attack order to the armored divisions poised on the Polish border. Actually, that wasn't the case in the beginning, according to Alexei. At the outset, Von Rundstedt's Army Group South, heading for southern Russia and the priceless oil fields of the Caucasus, had run into stiffer resistance in the Ukraine than either of the other two German spearheads driving through Byelorussia (White Russia) for Moscow and Leningrad. But now the *Panzerkorps* had broken through and rolled half-way across the Ukraine in less than six weeks. Rumor had it that the reeling Russians would attempt to make a major stand on the east bank of the Dnieper—*another* major stand, as Alexei put it.

"And why would they start shooting?" I scoffed at Georgi, anxious to regain my brother's approval. "It will be hours before the Germans get here," and I jerked my thumb in the direction of the steppes behind us. Covered with fast-ripening wheat as far as the eye could see, they stretched away to the horizon like a vast, becalmed sea, disturbed only by occasional ribbons of wind. No distant column of warships plowed the golden waves to signal the approach of the invader.

But again my estimate of what would please my brother proved wrong. Instead of joining with me in contempt of Georgi's query, he took it seriously, and with chagrin I realized that, of course, a good field commander must be prepared for every contingency.

"If they open fire while we're still up here, we will drop into the creek below and use the gully for cover to get back to the village." As he spoke these words, I happened to glance to my left towards the village—just as a grassy hummock atop the cliff suddenly disappeared. My mouth fell open; it was there, and then it wasn't. Gone in a geyser of dirt. From the shrubs and trees around it, leaves and limbs started falling to the ground, like a terrific wind was shaking them.

I tried to shout, but no sound would come from my throat. From the look on Alexei's face, I assumed that he had seen it, too, except that *he* was jabbing his finger at the *far* riverbank! And there I saw the face of the forest erupting in white smoke and flashes of fire.

Then the sound reached us—a rolling crescendo of multiple machine-gun fire, studded with heavier reports from field pieces. We could hardly hear above the din, and Alexei pointed downward: time to bail out. But the creek below seemed a long ways down and awfully shallow, and neither Georgi nor I made any move to leave our perches. Again, Alexei jammed his finger earthward, but I shook my head. I was remembering another fall into water . . . the terror of that wide-awake nightmare of the winter before caused me to cling to the limb I was on for dear life.

But when we heard whipping, sizzling sounds in the air around us, and leaves and twigs began to descend on us, without another thought I sprang out from the limb I was on, to clear those below. The surface of the creek rushed up and hit me in the chest, knocking my breath out. That, coupled with the shock of the cold water, brought back all the terror of the previous January, but Alexei shouted at me and, in the relative shelter of the gully, I could hear him. The three of us clambered out of the creek and flattened ourselves against the side of the gully that was most protected from the fusillade. Moryak was nowhere to be seen.

In addition to occasional artillery, there were also *Katushas* now—"Little Kates," the multiple, anti-tank rockets whose explosions sounded like a string of giant firecrackers. Just then, a shell landed inside the gully, back at the mouth behind us. The earth shook, and the concussion pressed us into the side of the gully, covering us with a film of dirt.

"We'll stay put until dark," Alexei said, his voice beginning to quaver.

"What'll we do then?" sobbed Georgi, who had given in to what all of us felt.

"I—I don't know." Alexei's voice broke, and he turned quickly away.

All of a sudden, my own fear vanished; somehow, I knew everything was going to be all right. In fact, I could even take an academic interest in what was going on overhead.

"Why *are* they shooting, if there aren't any Germans around?" I asked Alexei, and for once he seemed grateful for the question.

"Because the Russians don't know that," he explained, his voice steadying down. "The bank on our side of the river is so much higher than theirs, they can't see anything beyond the rim of the cliff and the tops of the houses."

"But aren't they wasting an awful lot of ammunition? I mean, those machine-guns have hardly let up since they started, and it seems like they've been firing for half an hour." And Georgi and I moved closer, to hear what he would say.

"Ever see a small dog in a house, when a big dog comes sniffing around outside?" Alexei continued. "The little dog will bark his head off, sounding like he would tear the big dog to pieces, if he could only get at him. Why? Because he knows he's safe, at least for the moment. He's trying to intimidate that bigger dog, who hasn't seen him yet, and probably more than anything, he's trying to encourage himself. That's what's going on over there."

I laughed, and even Georgi stopped whimpering.

"And if what we heard yesterday is right," I added, "then those are green officers who have never seen action. But aren't they worried about hitting civilians?"

Alexei turned to me, so full of scorn that he could hardly speak. "Vasili, you must have grown up with your head in a bucket! We're not civilians; we are *Ukrainians!*" And he spat the word out in imitation of a contemptuous Russian commisar.

We fell silent then, and listened to the guns, each wrapped in his own thoughts. As shadows began to form on the opposite side of the gully, I noted that the only place my pants were still clammy was where I was sitting down. My mind went back nine months to that other time that I had gone into the water with all my clothes on. . . .

It had been Sunday, and word had come that there were fish on the lake below the new dam, a half hour's walk from where we lived. At first I had thought they meant that people were ice-fishing, and I went to find the big wooden mallet and the ax. When there was new ice, clear of snow and not too thick, you could see through it, and when a fish happened to swim near enough, you took the mallet and gave the ice a terrific whack. The shock would stun the fish, and all you had to do was chop out the ice and scoop up your fish.

But it turned out that this was something else. The dam had broken at the top, and water was cascading onto the ice below. So were fish, who were then finding themselves stranded on top of the ice. At this news, Alexei and I hurriedly wrapped our feet in rags (most of the year we went barefoot, but in the dead of winter the temperature went to thirty or forty below zero and stayed there). My sister Lida wanted to come, too, but at three she was too little and would have to stay home with Babunia, mother's grandmother. My father was away again—he was away most of the time—so it would just be mother and Alexei and me.

By the time we got to the lake, it seemed like half the village was there ahead of us. And sure enough, it was simply a question of going out on the ice and picking up the fish where they lay—the easiest fishing I'd ever heard of! In no time we had four, which, if we boiled the heads and tails, would feed all of us, even the cat, for several days. Mother put them in a sack and took them home to prepare them, while Alexei and I went back out to see if we could find some more.

Such was my exhilaration at the prospect of fresh meat, after what seemed like an endless succession of potatoes and onions and beets, that I forgot the one hazard of this new type of fishing—thin ice, almost impossible to spot under the water from the dam that had not had time to freeze. The next thing I knew, I was up to my neck in water so cold that at first I could not even breathe. Then paddling like a dog to the edge of the ice, I tried to get up on it, but it kept breaking off under me, and I would fall back in. I tried as hard as I could to keep my head above water, but my clothes were heavy on me, pulling me down, and my arms and legs felt like rock. I went under.[1]

The last thing I remembered was looking up at the ice from underneath it—ice everywhere. . . . And then I seemed to see myself falling into a pit. I was falling for the longest time, tumbling into darkness, till I finally landed on my back at the bottom. It was like being at the bottom of a deep, deep well. From where I lay, it seemed that the pit spiraled upward and got narrower at the top, which was so far away that it was like looking through a gun barrel and seeing a tiny circle of light.

There was nothing else to do but to start climbing, only the dirt of the walls kept breaking off and piling up around and under me. And then that dirt began to move, and I discovered to my horror that I was not alone. Huge snakes,

---

1. Later, my mother told me that about an hour after this, there had been a knock at the door, and a man from the village, Dimitri Mikhailovich, stood there with me in his arms. "Here is your drowned, frozen son," was all he could say, and they laid me on the family table.

their bodies as big around as my thigh, were coiling themselves around me, trying to squeeze the life out of me. Some were black, and some were gray, and their skin had a sleek, dull sheen to it, as they compressed ever tighter around me.

They had me completely immobilized; I could not even breathe. But for some reason they seemed unable to wrap themselves around my head. At that moment, I somehow got an arm loose and grabbed at the dirt on the wall. It came away in my fingers, but it startled the snakes, and they momentarily loosed their grip. Quickly I pulled partly free and started hauling myself up toward the light. My one thought was to reach the top and get out in the sunshine, and on that thought I set my will, and it became the whole focus of my being.

But more snakes coiled around me, clear up to my chin, and they just pulled my feet out from under me and tumbled me back into the slime at the bottom. The fall shook us all, and this time I was able to get completely free for an instant. With that scant lead, I started up what looked like a shaft to the top.

Almost immediately they were back, fastening onto my legs and pulling at me, but I dug my fingers into the wall of the shaft and heaved upward. The dirt was hard-packed now, and my fingers soon felt like all the flesh was worn away from them, and I was holding on with the stubs of bones. Yet at each handhold, some dirt would come loose, and this dirt had the effect of distracting the snakes so that they relaxed their suffocating hold.

So much of my life had been given to just surviving that I instinctively took advantage of the slightest edge. I began to dig furiously, like a dog, showering the snakes behind me with dirt, and in so doing, not only did I manage to keep them off me, but I built up a foundation of dirt on which to stand.

Then, just as it looked like I might finally make it to the top and out into the sunlight, other snakes appeared out of nowhere, pinned my arms to my sides, and flung me to the bottom of the pit. And I had to begin all over again.

This time, as I approached the top, my strength was finished. This had to be it; if I fell back down again, there would be no starting over. With a last desperate effort, I lunged for the rim of the pit. And caught it. And pulled myself up and over it, kicking free of the most tenacious snake.

The sunlight hurt my eyes, and I had to squint, but I seemed to be on the side of a hill, overlooking the Dnieper River, not far from where we lived. Gasping for breath, I wanted to stop and rest, but the snakes were boiling up out of the pit behind me, so I started up the hill to get away from them. At first, my body seemed still partially paralyzed, and I could only crawl.

The fastest snake caught me then, wrapped itself around my leg, and began to pull me back towards the pit, but by that time enough strength had returned so that I could kick free of him. I lurched to my feet, staggered a few steps forward, and fell and got up and tried again. It seemed that the closer I got to the top of the hill, the brighter was the sunlight. And I noticed that apparently the snakes didn't like the light. All but the biggest of them had turned back, and at the very top, which I had just reached, it was so bright that none of the snakes could stand it. I sank down to the ground, sobbing for breath, and just lay there on my back in the sun, my eyes closed . . . until, far away, I seemed to hear someone speaking my name.

two

My eyes fluttered open, and I was lying on my back, wrapped in a blanket on the family table. And there was Babunia, with one hand resting on my feet and the other raised in the air. She seemed to be looking up at it, except that her eyes were closed, and she was speaking softly, in a way I had never heard before.

I must have stirred, because her eyes opened and looked down into mine. "Vasili? He's *alive!*" And she redoubled whatever it was she was saying, punctuating it with laughter and tears and thanks to God. Just then, my mother came out of the other room, red-eyed and wondering what all the commotion was about. And she, too, started laughing and crying and dancing about. And Alexei and Lida joined in, too.

I sat up on the edge of the table, shook my head, and rubbed my eyes. The pit and the snakes . . . where were they? And what were Babunia and mother and the others

23

doing? What a sight they made, whirling around the room in the flickering light from the fire in the open, mud-brick oven! The people in our village hardly ever laughed; in fact, about the only time they laughed at all was at weddings, and then it was a wild, almost sad thing, and only after downing a lot of *samagonka*—home-made vodka. But here were my mother and Babunia, cavorting around and hugging me—so happy that it made them cry.

"What's the matter? What are you *doing?*" I shouted, almost angry.

My mother hugged me and leaned back, looking me in the eye, her own eyes shining. "When Dimitri Mikhailovich brought you in—that was long before dark—you were frozen. Your lips were blue, your clothes were solid ice, and you were not breathing; you hadn't been, since they fished you out." She paused. "Now you are!" And she was off again; so were the others, and we had as much fun that night as a family as we had ever had.

The next morning, before I went to school, Babunia took me aside and had a very serious talk with me. "Vasili, you must never tell anyone about what happened last night. No one," she paused to let the words sink in. "Some day, when you are older, I will explain it to you. Until then, not a word, understand?"

I nodded gravely. I suspected that it had something to do with God, because the only other time she had ever spoken to me that way was when I had told her what had happened to me in school one day. One of the boys in my class had earlier asked the teacher who God was, and that day she had prepared an object lesson.

"Stalin is the sunshine," she said, pointing to his picture. "And Uncle Lenin gives us all the good things in our life. There is no God, no kind old grandfather up in the sky with a great white beard. To prove it, I want you all to pray now to God, and ask Him for something—something good to eat—ask Him for some candy, why don't you?"

We all dutifully bowed our heads and clasped our hands, as she had demonstrated. Nothing happened. After letting us wait until we could hardly sit still another moment, our teacher then said, "Now pray to Uncle Lenin. Ask *him* for some candy, and see what happens."

Again, we bowed our heads, and almost immediately the classroom door burst open, and in danced a young woman in a white, ballerina-like costume, flinging a couple of hand-fuls of hard candies all over the schoolroom. Pandemonium broke out, as we scrambled over one another after the candy. Our teacher had to shout to make herself heard: *"You see what happens when you pray to Lenin?"*

When we were finally back at our desks, and things had calmed down somewhat, I felt compelled to say what was on my mind: "But there *is* a God. And He lives in heaven. Babunia says so!"

"And who is that?" our teacher asked, her eyes narrow-ing.

"She's my mother's grandmother," I almost whispered, realizing too late that I had made a great mistake.

"Well, she probably never went to school herself and lost what wits she had long before you were born. Imagine, believing such fairy stories!" And she made a joke of it, encouraging the rest of the class to join in.

"But, just so you don't forget," she added, when the laughter died, "I want you to go in that corner, face the wall, and kneel and pray to that God of your great-grandmother's for the rest of the afternoon. And to give you something to pray about, I want you to roll up your pants and kneel on these," and she spread some hard, dried peas in the corner. They cut into my knees, and as much as I wanted to cry, I was not going to let the teacher or the others know how much it hurt.

That night, when I told Babunia what had happened, she

was, just for a moment, afraid. It was the only time I had ever seen her that way, and somehow I knew that it was me she was afraid for, not for herself. "Never mention heaven or God again, to anyone! And don't ask me to tell you about them!"

"But why? I love it when you tell—"

"Because the Communists hate God and Jesus Christ. And if they hear you talking about them, they could do bad things to us—much worse than kneeling on peas.[1] I wanted

---

1. A quarter of a century later, Alexsandr Solzhenitsyn would document what Babunia had known only by intuition: "the root destruction of religion in the country, which throughout the twenties and thirties was one of the most important goals of the GPU-NKVD, could be realized only by mass arrests. . . . Monks and nuns, whose black habits had been a distinctive feature of Old Russian life, were intensively rounded up on every hand, placed under arrest, and sent into exile. They arrested and sentenced active laymen. The circles kept getting bigger, as they raked in ordinary believers as well, old people, and particularly women, who were the most stubborn believers of all and who, for many long years to come, would be called 'nuns' in transit prisons and in camps.

"True, they were supposedly being arrested and tried not for their actual faith but for openly declaring their convictions and for bringing up their children in the same spirit. . . . A person convinced that he possessed spiritual truth was required to conceal it from his own children! In the twenties, the religious education of children was classified as a political crime under Article 58–10, of the Code—in other words, counter-revolutionary propaganda!" (*The Gulag Archipelago*, Harper & Row, 1973, pp. 37-38.)

By the thirties, the prevalent practice was simply to remove the child from his family, to be raised "in a more suitable, State-oriented environment." (It is ironic that the philosopher who had the most influence on Marx and Lenin, where the deification of the State was concerned, also had the most influence on Hitler.

to ask why they hated them, but I could tell from Babunia's tone that I'd better not ask any more questions, if I wanted a story that night.

Each night, just before Alexei and I went to sleep, we would curl up on the straw-covered floor in front of the open oven, on either side of Babunia, and she would tell us a story, moving her fingers lightly through our hair in a way that would sometimes put us to sleep before the story was over. We would gaze at the scrap of wood or dried dung that was burning in the oven, and our imaginations would dance with princes and firebirds and enchanted frogs and water sprites and far-away kingdoms. Always the person that we wanted to win, or marry the princess, did, though it was sometimes an awfully close thing. It was our sole form of entertainment (though we were learning to read, our family owned no books), and we wouldn't have traded it for anything, because here—and only here, in these stories of Babunia's—did things turn out the way they were supposed to.

I asked Babunia one night how she came to know so many, for it seemed like she could go on indefinitely without repeating herself, unless we specifically requested one of our favorites. She told us that she had learned them as a child from her own grandmother, and that her favorites turned out to be ours, too. And then she told us the real-life story of her own childhood.

Babunia was not her real name—it means "grandmother"—but it was the only name I ever knew her by. Her family had been well-to-do, as had my father's. They owned considerable property and livestock, and Babunia had a very happy early life. There was plenty of food in those

This was Hegel, the nineteenth-century Berlin professor who considered the State as the supreme achievement of mankind, "the highest revelation of the World-Spirit.")

days—plenty of everything for everyone, in fact. For while the Czar had demanded taxes, he had not deprived the people of almost all they produced, as the Communists did.

And the Ukrainians were superb farmers, on the most fertile soil in all Europe—a land so rich that it was nicknamed "the black earth." They were a people particularly close to that earth in an almost mystical way, with an uncanny gift for making things grow. To them, it was perfectly natural to speak soft, gentle words of encouragement to the young shoots of wheat and the potato and onion seeds that they carefully folded into the soil of their vegetable gardens. They gladly poured out their lives into their plants and crops, which seemed to respond in kind, and they had a profound, if not always articulate appreciation of the deep things of the spirit.

But they were also a proud, stubborn and fiercely independent people, who still regarded Kiev, not St. Petersburg or Moscow, as their capital, and who, like their ancestors, the Zaporozhye Cossacks, were notorious for submitting to no one. Such a man did Babunia grow up to marry—a giant of a forester who was also a superb wood-worker, and who was the strongest man she, or I, had ever heard of. When felling timber, instead of taking horses into the forest to drag the trees out, he and his two brothers, would bring them out themselves. After removing the limbs of a fallen tree his brothers would hoist the top end on their shoulders, while he alone would carry out the base.

For all his enormous strength, Babunia assured us, he was a gentle man, slow to anger. But when provoked to wrath, there was not a man alive who could stand up to him. With a single swipe of the back of his hand, he had permanently deafened one man, and with the tip of one finger, he had smashed flat the nose of another.

Babunia and her husband had two daughters, one of whom inherited none of my great-grandfather's strength and died not long after giving birth to my mother, who was thus raised mostly by her grandmother. Babunia did her best to bring little Maria up as a devout Christian—which was not easy to do after October, 1917, the month that permanently changed the lives of everyone east of Warsaw.

The Bolsheviks hated anyone who owned or worked land, and they took it all, putting in charge local men who had been the refuse of rural society—too lazy or too addicted to vodka to hold jobs. These men enjoyed their revenge upon those whom they fancied had "exploited" them, engaging in plunder, rape and even murder, and cloaking it all in the name of "revolutionary justice."

"And remember," Babunia had said, "some of these Bolsheviks were Ukrainians, *our own people*. The Russian commissars did not come until later."

She told us what they did to her husband's brother. First, they took all his land, animals and food supplies. Then they persuaded themselves that he must have a secret cache of grain. They began to torment him about it, and when he insisted that such a cache did not exist, they began to torture him, forcing hot needles under his fingernails, smashing his fingers in a door. And then they started in on his wife.

Finally, just to get them to stop, he "confessed" and took them to where he had lived, pointing to the floor. In a frenzy, they tore up the floor and the ground beneath it. There was nothing, of course, and they beat him senseless. When he came to, he pointed to a spot in the back yard, and they dug there. By the time they finally tired of their treasure hunt, the whole house was torn apart, and the yard was full of craters. In their fury, the Bolsheviks took him outside in the cold of mid-winter, tied him behind a sled and two horses, and dragged him around the town until he lost his mind and died.[2]

---

2. Ironically, most of the Bolsheviks were themselves subsequently accused of treason and imprisoned or executed, as the Communists assumed more and more central control of the Revolution. With the rise of Stalin to Party Secretary in 1929, the subjection of the Ukrainian people began in earnest. (It should be borne in mind that although Stalin had achieved absolute supremacy and would go to extraordinary lengths to retain it, had he not been in basic harmony with the Communist mind and will, an assassin's bullet would have abruptly curtailed his reign. And though in 1956, Party Secretary Khrushchev would denounce him and attempt to make him the scapegoat for all the evils perpetrated in the thirties and forties, the man was clearly the product of the system, and not the system of the man.)

It was Stalin's intent to industrialize the Soviet Union at once, and to do this he took millions of farmers off the land, brought them into the cities, and transformed them into factory workers. Then, in order to feed the suddenly swollen urban populations, he turned to the Ukraine. Collectivization had already been accomplished; now he fashioned it into an instrument with a dual purpose: to satiate the ravenous hunger of the cities and to break the Ukrainian will, once and for all time.

Having set food-production quotas high enough to virtually insure widespread famine—according to Solzhenitsyn, in *U.S. News and World Report* (July 14, 1975), six *million* Ukrainians starved to death in 1932 and 1933 alone—the Communists instituted a system of food rewards for informing, which instilled fear at such a deep level that a man dared not trust anyone, not even the members of his own family. In a land where food had always been so plentiful that no one gave it a thought, starvation became an ever-present spectre. (You might think that you would die sooner than turn in your neighbor for stealing food or making a negative comment, but when your own children have had nothing in their bellies for a week or two, you would be surprised at what you would do for a couple of kilos of flour.)

Alexei and I didn't care much for Babunia's real-life stories; nothing ever came out right in the end. But she seemed to think that they were things we needed to know and remember always, and they would often take the place of tales of magical kingdoms and cunning wolves that could talk like goats.

Babunia did not tell us much about our mother Maria's childhood. Times were hard under the Communists; the old way of life was made to seem archaic, bourgeois. It was all Babunia could do to keep her headstrong granddaughter in line, and the time came when she no longer could. In June of 1930, at the age of eighteen, Maria up and married a hard-eyed, hard-fisted roamer named Ivan Basansky, who was barely seventeen himself.

But about three years before that, something happened to both her and Babunia that was to profoundly affect the rest of their lives—and ours, too. Babunia never spoke of it, and mother only told us of it years afterwards.

Babunia had gone to one of her secret worship meetings and there had met a holy man from America,[3] and had had

---

Thus, while hundreds of thousands *were* being shipped off to the overcrowded labor camps of Siberia (the NKVD—we called it *chornaya vorona*, "black crow"—would come by night in black cars to whisk people away without trial. Lacking gas chambers in those early days they often herded their victims into river barges which they would then sink), it was not necessary to arrest and deport the entire Ukrainian population; they were prisoners where they were, and productive prisoners at that. This was Stalin's solution to "the Ukrainian problem."

3. This was the legendary Russian-American Baptist, who was called by God to take the message of a living, risen Savior and the enabling power of His Holy Spirit into Communist Russia. This he did, at great peril to his life, in underground meetings all across eastern Russia. Ultimately he was betrayed and died in a

her faith and her spiritual understanding immeasurably deepened. From that time forth, such a sense of peace and strength emanated from her that she was like a sturdy tree in a windstorm; you wanted to be as close to her as you could get.

Mother, too, at a later meeting, had had a similar experience. She had gone as a skeptic, really at Babunia's insistence, but when she saw people whom she knew could not read, open a Bible and suddenly be able to read from it, and prophesy things that only God could know, when she saw people miraculously healed from life-long physical defects, she became a believer.

But she was young and full of life, and her friends used to mock her for sneaking off to her silly prayer meetings (this was before the Communists had gained sufficient control to crack down hard on such meetings), and they encouraged her to come with them to dances instead. Against her grandmother's wishes she went, and it was at one of these dances that she met and fell in love with my father. They were married almost immediately, and in two years she had two children, both boys.

Unfortunately, Ivan Basansky was hardly ready to settle down. He was away almost all the time, either in jail or "traveling," and this meant that my mother had to work two shifts a day to earn enough labor points to get us through the winter. At 4:00 A.M., the *bregadier*, the leader of her labor-brigade, would rap on our window, and she would hurry out into the dark to work eight hours as a field cook. Then, in the afternoon, she would either man a plow behind two horses or do whatever farmwork needed to be

---

Siberian labor camp, but as a result of this one man's obedience, there are now many thousands of underground Christians behind the Iron Curtain.

done. Both jobs were men's jobs, for which she was grateful, because they were worth more points at the end of the growing season. Without those extra points, there was no way that all of us could make it through the winter. In the meantime, since only those who worked got fed, she would take half her portion home to feed the rest of us.

While she was working, Babunia looked after us. Most of the time we were in school, an hour's walk away, but in the summer, we helped Babunia tend the little vegetable patch that surrounded our house, and which provided the potatos and onions we took into the town of Belenkoye to sell, in order to buy clothes and shoes. Babunia was our tree, and we clung to her whenever it started to blow.

At the time, I knew nothing at all about the source of her strength, and she was careful to keep it that way, for a slip of my tongue could separate us forever. Nevertheless, I suspected that it had something to do with God, especially the times when three or four elderly women would make their way to our house at night. Babunia would put blankets over the windows and send Alexei and me outside, to keep watch and let them know if anyone was coming. I could not imagine what on earth they were doing, but I knew that if Babunia were doing it, it had to be all right.

The darkest time of my younger life was one evening when Babunia wasn't there. There was work available that she could do, and since I was only seven at the time, an older girl from a few houses away came and stayed with us. This girl enjoyed frightening us; she loved to tell us horror stories of the Duduj, "the bogeyman," till we were trembling with fear.

This particular evening, unbeknownst to us, she brought a little piglet with her, which she tied outside the window. She told us in a low voice, full of fear, that the Duduj had been seen in the next village and had left the picked-clean bones of a little boy of around seven on his parents' doorstep. But the Duduj had a voracious appetite and was never satisfied for very long, and when he was hungry, he would prowl around and scream with rage, until he could find another little boy to devour. Worst of all, you couldn't keep him out by locking the door, because he was magic.

At this point in her story, her eyes widened, and she looked towards the window. "Did you hear something?" she whispered. Both of us shook our heads, not daring to breathe. She put her finger to her lips and motioned us to be perfectly still—as if we were about to go anywhere. Then she slowly got to her feet and eased out the front door.

She must have done something to the piglet, because it suddenly started screaming. She burst in the door and slammed it behind her, shouting, "It's the Duduj! He's *here! Right outside that window!*" And our own screams drowned out those of the pig's.

Later that night, when Babunia came home, she got very angry at the girl, and did her best to assure us that it was just pretend, but from that time on, I began having nightmares about the Duduj coming after me. These dreams seemed to increase in intensity, till one night in my sleep I ran outside, and Babunia had to chase me a long ways through the snow before she could catch me and wake me up.

From then on, I was also paralyzed with fear whenever I heard a pig squeal. One Sunday, my mother was taking some grain to a neighbor's house to thresh, and I went with her. It was dark inside that house and, coming in from the bright sun, I couldn't see a thing. They had a pig in there unbeknownst to me, on the other side of a partition. There was some straw over boards where we went in, and as we entered, the pig let out a squeal. I screamed and jumped up in the air, and when I came down, a big, rusty nail went all the way up through my right foot.

Screaming, I lifted up my foot. The board dangled from it, and mother pulled the nail out. I was bleeding all over the place, and she carried me home. There was no medication for such a thing, and no doctor nearer than Zaporozhye, fifty kilometers away, so there was little she could do but hope that somehow it would be all right.

But it wasn't. Already red and swollen, my foot now became infected and the pain unbearable. Blood poisoning began to spread through my body and I was soon burning with fever. To draw the poison out, Babunia packed the wound with cow dung so fresh that it was still warm, and laying her hand on the foot, she closed her eyes and began to move her lips.

I sensed what she was doing had something to do with God, and it made me feel better, but the whole lower leg was now swollen. That night, I overheard mother asking Babunia if it wouldn't be better to cut off the leg rather than let me die. Babunia made no answer; exchanging the dung for a poultice of raw potatoes to draw out the pus, she covered this with leaves from the bearclaw plant and again bowed her head and closed her eyes. Again, my mother asked about cutting off the leg, and this time Babunia looked up and shook her head—and smiled. And eventually my foot healed.

But not my fear of the Duduj—not until the night after the Russians left. Mother was home for a change; the Commissar and his staff of overseers had left several days before the army, clearly afraid of what the Germans (or the people of our village) might do to them. Even so, it had taken a couple of days for the people to realize that they no longer had to work from two hours before sunrise till two hours after sunset.

Mother didn't have to get up in the middle of the night, and that alone was reason enough to celebrate. From deep in the keep-hole in the back yard (a shaft which went down eight meters or so and had tunnels at various levels to keep things cool in summer and above freezing in winter), we fetched some salt pork that we had been saving for a special occasion. To it we added potatoes and onions and beets, and as a second treat, sauerkraut with apples in it. And when everything was ready, as the best surprise of all, Babunia produced hot, steaming black barley bread! It was the finest meal I could ever remember.

Afterwards, we put one of our precious winter logs on the fire, even though it wasn't really that cold, and we lit the grease lamp, which we hardly ever used.

"Would you like to hear a story?" Babunia asked, and all of us shouted *da!*

"Well, the Communists are gone," she said, in solemn tones, "and the Germans will soon be here, so this may be the last night that things will ever be like this again. Tonight I am going to tell you the story of the Land of Milk and Honey." And so saying, she brought forth a huge book, bound in black leather that gleamed softly in the lamplight. I was astonished; not only had I not known that they made books that big, I thought I knew every cranny of our little three-room house and could not imagine where she had been keeping it.

This gray-haired, bony-figured little woman, who was then in her seventies, seated herself on the straw by the firelight of the open oven, her back straight and her eyes clear—almost like one's imagination of royalty. And as usual, we gathered around her, though each of us and mother, too, sensed that tonight was somehow different.

"This is a real-life story," Babunia went on, and noting the disappointment that flickered across our faces, she added, "but it is a story that happens in the future, not the past—your own future, each one of you. As you listen to it, remember that it's true, every bit of it. It's all written right here,". and with a thin forefinger she tapped the large book that lay open on her lap. "When it's over, see if you don't think it's the best story you've ever heard."

Hardly convinced, we nonetheless settled ourselves in the straw and got comfortable. Lida was already nodding off to sleep. Milk and honey—I tried to recall when I had last had some milk. All I could remember was that I hadn't gotten nearly enough of it. As for honey, I had never tasted any, but Babunia said it was sweeter and better than anything I ever had tasted, even melted sugar.

The Land of Milk and Honey was another name for the place called heaven, where God lived with His Son, Jesus, and where everyone who loved them would go when they died. There was no darkness in heaven, just sunshine everywhere, but you could always find shade under a tree. Between the trees grew tall, green grass, and a slight breeze would bend it to and fro. There was a valley in heaven, and in the distance, mountains sheltered it on both sides. It was easily the most beautiful place there ever was.

Through this valley flowed a gentle river. The water was so clear and so warm that you could go swimming in it and never get too cold or too hot. And it somehow made you so buoyant that you didn't ever have to kick or move your arms to stay on the surface. If you were exhausted, all you had to do was get in the river and float, and you would be be completely refreshed.

Both banks of the river were lined with trees, whose limbs hung low over the water and were laden with fruit—oranges and apples and pears and something called plums, and other fruit that I had never heard of. (I knew what oranges were; my father had brought two home with him once and given them to Alexei and me. An orange was such a rare thing that I felt I really should memorize what it looked and tasted like, so that I would always be able to tell people that I had actually had one and to describe it in detail. I studied that orange day after day, even taking it to sleep with me. Finally, when I felt I knew its shape and color by heart, it was time to eat it. But when I did cut it open, it had turned rotten inside, and I never did learn what it tasted like.)

There was, of course, no hunger in heaven; whenever you felt like having something to eat, all you had to do was reach up into one of the trees—the fruit was so ripe that just the heat from the palm of your hand was enough to cause the fruit to fall into it. And by the time you had eaten that piece, another would have grown in its place. When you bit into the fruit, the sweet goodness of it was like nothing you had ever tasted. As Babunia came to this part, I could see myself eating that fruit; I could taste it and feel its goodness sliding down my throat and into my stomach. And I got excited, because I seemed to be actually experiencing it; it seemed like life was going down into me!

Babunia was right, of course: it *was* the best story that we had ever heard! More real than real-life and yet more fabulous than any make-believe. Somehow, I sensed, the story itself had *done* something. Something was different after it—and because of it. (Months later, I would happen to notice that my fear of the Duduj was gone, and when I thought about it, I realized that, after the story of the Land of Milk and Honey, that fear had never returned.)

The Land of Milk and Honey . . . I rubbed my empty stomach and listened almost contentedly to the seemingly muted staccato of machine-gun fire. Something out of the corner of my eye caught my attention, and I glanced up, startled to see a human form, bent low, hurtling down the gully towards us.

three

It was my father! But it couldn't be! Alexei had said he was up north, in one of the armies defending Kiev. Yet here he came, and Moryak was with him. And though he ran in a crouch, every so often his head would bob above the rim of the gully, and almost immediately spurts of dirt would kick up along the rise behind where his head had just been.

Alexei was watching, too. "Someone over there has a pair of field glasses and is directing that gun's fire!" he shouted. "Now they *must* be convinced that the Germans have arrived!" And sure enough, all along the line, the firing suddenly intensified.

"Alexei! Vasili!" father yelled as he came. "Keep down!" As if we had any intention of doing anything else.

Reaching the three of us, he threw himself against the near side of the gully and struggled for breath. My feelings were in a turmoil: part of me was glad to see him, grateful that he had come for us; the other part dreaded the sight of him. But before I could sort out what I felt, Alexei asked, "Father, what are you doing here?"

Our father looked at him for a moment before answering. "I and a few others were lucky enough to escape from the Uman encirclement. The Germans came from the north, down through Belaya Tserkov and Novo Arkhangelsk; from the west, through Vinnitsa; and from the south, across the Dniester. They closed the circle at Pervomaysk, and I heard they took more than one hundred thousand prisoners."

He stopped for breath, and to see how we were taking what he said. "The Sixth, Twelfth and Eighteenth Armies were smashed," he clapped his hands together and held them out to us, palms up. "They simply do not exist any more. I tried to cross the Dneiper, to be re-assigned, but they've blown all the bridges. And as you can see," he added, gesturing in the direction of the far shore, "they're shooting at anything that moves. So, here I am."

"But father," persisted Alexei, "we heard that Stalin had given the order: 'Stand fast and die.' And if a hundred thousand prisoners *were* taken, how come—"

"Listen!" our father hissed, "We were issued one rifle for every fifty men! And three bullets for each rifle! You think that's going to stop the Panzerkorps?" His eyes narrowed. "Or maybe you'd be happier if I were starving to death in some German prisoner-of-war camp?"

Alexei and I knew it was time to keep silent. After the Duduj, my father was the main source of fear in my life—a real, known source. Such was his temper that, though not that large, he would take on someone twice his size in an instant, if he thought he had been crossed in any way. He feared no man, "not even the devil himself," as Babunia would say. Not even Babunia's husband, though until the latter died of a fever, my father used to sleep with a knife under his mattress, in case he should ever come after him.

And there was a good chance that that might happen, because my father was also the meanest man I ever knew. Whenever he did come home, he was usually drunk, and he would either beat us up or my mother, when she came home from work. One day, he beat her so badly that she stood, bent double, blood flowing from her ears and nose.

I ran outside screaming, trying to get someone to stop him, before he killed her. But those whom I saw either went on as if they hadn't heard me, or they just laughed at me—in the new Russia, contrary to propaganda, the men consider themselves definitely superior beings. Women are there primarily to satisfy them, and any man who doesn't beat his wife from time to time is less than a man. My father was even more manly; he beat Babunia too, but only after her husband was safely in the ground.

The most frightening thing about my father's rages was that he beat us for no discernible reason. If you spoke to him, he'd beat you for that; if you didn't, he'd beat you for that. If you moved while he was hitting you, he'd beat you the harder. And if you didn't move, that so incensed him that he was likely to tie you to a post and whip you like an animal, with one of the bullwhips he liked to make. When he did that, you couldn't take your shirt off afterwards, because it would be stuck in the grooves in your skin.

It was even worse, if that was possible, when you did give him a reason. One spring, Alexei and I had gone down to the Dnieper and were throwing stones in the water. Alexei got his *valenki* wet—his new, heavy felt boots that father had just bought for him. When father learned of it, he screamed and grabbed Alexei, hoisting him over his head like a sack of potatoes and flinging him on the ground—so hard that Alexei's lungs were torn loose from his rib cage, and he very nearly died.

One evening, while my father was away, I asked Babunia why he was the way he was, when she and mother were so different. She looked into the fire and pursed her lips before answering: "In the olden days, they used to say that if a man were bitter and hated enough, an evil spirit would come into him and possess him." Something in my expression must have told Babunia how hard I found that to accept. "Well," she said, with a smile and a shrug, "*kto znaet*—who can say? There's no question he'd had plenty to be bitter about." And that night, we heard the real-life story of Ivan Savielevich Basansky.

Like my mother Maria's family, Ivan's were *Kulaki*, well-to-do farmers. For generations they had had more than a hundred hectares of forest and fields, stables, and servants to see to their every need. The fact that their name ended in y, instead of i, had the same significance as the prefix von before a German name, a sign of aristocracy.

Ivan was barely five, that day in the fall of 1917, when the Bolsheviks pounded on his family's door and informed them that they had one hour to gather their belongings and clear off "the people's property." But their belongings did not include horses or wagons; they too, belonged to "the people." Due to the upheaval that swept the land during harvest time, or perhaps to God's displeasure, there was a crop failure that fall, which was followed by an extremely severe winter. All across the snowbound steppes famine raged, and the thousands of former land-owners who had been turned out of their homes had no food, or even work or shelter, for those who still had their homes were afraid to employ them, much less take them in. They made do the best they could, but it was not long before a typhoid epidemic decimated their ranks.

When Ivan's parents, weakened by hunger and the extreme cold, caught the fever and died, such was the fear of

entire German Sixth Army was encircled. It held out for seven weeks, despite the fact that the *Luftwaffe* was able to deliver less than twenty per cent of the air support that Goering had promised.

Finally, on January 31, 1943, out of ammunition, food, fuel, and medical supplies, and against the direct order of the Fuhrer, what remained of the Sixth Army surrendered. Ninety-one thousand officers and men were taken prisoner, and nearly twice that many remained behind, buried in the deep snows of the Russian steppes. It was the worst defeat in German military history and the turning-point of the war.

In our village the climate changed quickly after that. The first thing that happened was that the dreaded, black uniformed SS came in and took over all occupation functions from the too-lenient Wehrmacht. My father, as usual, was one of the first to see the handwriting on the wall. He urged us to come with him and get completely out of the country, but mother was not yet ready to abandon the known, as bad as it was, for the unknown. And so, in a fit of anger, father went alone.

Now the orders for the subjugation of the *Untermenschen*—the subhumans, as the Nazi geopolitical theorists dubbed the Slavic peoples—were carried out to the letter.[4]

---

4. Many of these top-secret directives were issued *before* Hitler broke his non-aggression pact with Stalin on June 22, 1941. A sampling from them indicates the tenor of the Nazis' attitude.

"The war against Russia will be such that it cannot be conducted in knightly fashion. This struggle is one of ideologies and racial differences and will have to be conducted with unprecedented, unmerciful and unrelenting harshness. . . . Commissars will be liquidated. . . . German soldiers guilty of breaking international law will be excused."   —*Adolph Hitler,* March, 1941

"The job of feeding the German people stands at the top of the list of Germany's claims on the East. The southern (Ukrainian)

All pretense of beneficence was dropped. The Germans were the conquerors, we the conquered. Unhampered by having to maintain a semblance of representing the people's interests, as the Communists had had to before them, the Nazis' arrogance was supreme. On March 5, in Kiev, Erich Koch, Reich Commissar for the Ukraine, expressed it unequivocally in a public speech for all to hear:

"We are the Master Race and must govern hard but just . . . I will draw the very last out of this country. . . . The population must work, work, and work again. . . . We definitely did not come here to give out manna. We have come here to create the basis for victory.

"We are a Master Race, which must remember that the lowest German worker is racially and biologically a thousand times more valuable then the population here."

What the SS lacked in their predecessors' understanding of the Ukrainian soul, they more than made up for in the ruthlessness of their methods. They soon set up their own network of informers, and before long the odor of fear was again abroad in the land, until, as Babunia had long ago predicted, Communist or Fascist, there was not a choice between them.

Any hope that the pressure might once again be alleviated by the success of the German's summer offensive soon vanished. By the summer of 1943, Germany's capacity to carry the war to the enemy had so diminished that they were incapable of mounting any kind of an offensive until

---

territories will have to serve. . . . We see absolutely no reason for any obligation on our part to feed also the Russian Ukrainian people with the products of that surplus territory. We know that this is a harsh necessity, bare of any feelings. . . . The future will hold very hard years in store for the Russians."
—Alfred Rosenberg, *Commissioner for the Central Control of the East Europe Region.* June 20, 1941 (from William Shirer's *The Rise and Fall of the Third Reich,* Simon and Shuster, 1960, pp. 832-22).

July 5, two months late. It lasted exactly one week. From that point on, the momentum shifted to—and stayed with—the Russians. All of us knew then, that it was just a matter of time, and the Germans knew we knew it, which only made matters worse. The curtain was ringing down on the Thousand Year Reich, 990 years ahead of schedule. But there was no private rejoicing in the Ukraine; the alternative awaiting us was hardly something to shout, or even whisper, about.

About the time of that year's harvest, I had a dream, the most vivid that I had had since dreaming of the snake pit three years before. In the dream I went to the door of our house and saw a vast column of people passing by. I recognized some of them as people of our village, but there were many, many more, stretching all the way to the southern horizon. At first I wanted to hurry and join the column, except that they didn't look very happy, and something made me try to see where they were headed.

To the north and west, the sky at the horizon was aflame. In my dream the horizon was foreshortened so that I could see that it was actually an abyss. I could not see what lay beyond the edge, but into the sky showered spurts of fiery liquid, like bubbles bursting in a crucible of molten steel.

As those at the front of the column approached the edge of the abyss, they would start screaming, and their last screams would die away as each went over the edge. And another bubble would burst. I was terrified, and knowing that they would be looking for me in the house, I ran outside. In front of the house we had a little picket style fence, and I hid behind this, opening the gate and pulling it as close behind me as possible. I was so scared, I squeezed my eyes shut and tried not to breathe.

When I opened them, I was looking at the ground through the fence—at two huge feet. There were sandals on them, and the thongs that laced up the calves were as thick as my little finger. I quickly closed my eyes and opened them again, but the feet and legs were still there. My eyes traveled up to the knees behind a white robe; those knees were above the top of the fence, which meant that the man they belonged to had to be twice as tall as a man could be!

It was a long time before I dared look any higher, and all the while, the feet never moved. Finally, I looked up to the face—deeply tanned, with a full, dark brown beard and blue eyes. The eyes were not windows to anger but to compassion, full of sorrow and gentleness and patience and even a touch of humor. The moment I looked into them, all fear left me.

The man reached down to me, and I took his hand with both of mine. He led me out from behind the gate and to my joy, in the direction opposite that which the column was taking. Then I knew that I did not have to go with the others, that this man was big enough to take me away from the abyss, and I clung to his hand as tightly as I could. And I woke up.

When I told Babunia the dream and asked her what it meant, she wouldn't tell me. But it made her very, very happy.

PART TWO

five

"*Raus!*" The shouted command was followed by a short burst of machine-gun fire, very close. All of us rushed to the window to see what was happening. It was raining out, under a heavy overcast, and there were Germans everywhere, more than we'd ever seen before. They were pounding on doors with their rifle butts and occasionally firing their submachine guns in the air, ordering the people out and herding them into a column that was rapidly forming in the road.

Already they were next door; there was no time to think or even breathe. "Quick!" mother yelled, "Get your boots on and your warmest clothes!" As we raced to do just that, we could hear the woman next door screaming that she couldn't go; she was about to give birth. But it made no difference. Her husband had a hand cart, and they heaved her up on it.

Our door flew open, a man in a long grey coat and black

69

helmet gestured with his rifle for us to get outside fast. And we all tumbled down the path and into the road.

"Wait! Where's Babunia?" I cried and turned to go back in, but the soldier behind me shook his head. *"Raus! Raus!"*

"No! I've *got* to get Babunia!" He calmly pointed his rifle at me, and I saw his finger go around the trigger. I didn't care; I would rather die than leave Babunia behind. But just then, mother started screaming my name from the road, and reluctantly I turned and went to her.

"Don't worry," she said, fighting back tears, "she'll be all right." But neither one of us believed that.

After a day of slogging through the mud and rain, we had made barely five kilometers. No one was permitted to stop to help those who had keeled over from exhaustion, and those who tried to carry or support others soon fell by the wayside themselves. It was all we could do to spell mother from time to time in carrying Lida, who was slung in a blanket on her back. The Germans assigned to escort the convoy were obviously displeased with our progress, and so there was no stopping at dusk. Not that there was anything to stop *for*—none of us had brought any food, and they certainly weren't about to provide any. Or water—if you wanted a drink, you looked for a rainfilled footprint where the mud hadn't caved in.

The rain itself had stopped, and a dense, clammy fog filled the valley we were in. During a brief pause in the march (the Germans themselves had to rest), mother called us close to her. "Now listen carefully: I know this valley. I used to play here when I was your age. There are caves big enough for us to hide in, not five hundred meters from where we're standing right now. Do exactly as I tell you: ease away to the left, as if you were going to relieve yourself, then go another ten steps and stand still. The fog will cover you, and I'll find you."

From what I could see of the column in the dusk, everything was quiet. Everyone was sitting down, oblivious to the mud, and many had fallen asleep right where they sat. A little ahead of where we were, and to the right, three German guards were huddled together on a bit of higher ground, smoking. They had about a half a cigarette to go, which gave us about three minutes.

We did as mother had instructed us, and just about the time we heard the column getting to its feet, she materialized out of the fog, a slightly darker silhouette in the gathering dusk. Lida was on her back, and putting her finger on my lips and then on Alexei's, she had us join hands then took my other hand—it was that easy to get lost in the fog. Two wrong steps, and the only way we could have gotten back together again would have been to stand still and holler. Yet, incredibly, with only a few misturns, we arrived at the mouth of a cave that was big enough to get into without having to crawl.

As we started into the pitch-black cave, we heard something inside and froze in our tracks. Whatever was inside froze, too, and we listened to each other listening. Finally, when we could not have stood it another moment, we heard a little baby start to cry, and mother sighed. "It's others like us." .

It turned out there were four other families already in the cave, two from our village and two from other villages in the Dnieper bend. Inside the cave, it was almost more wet than outside, with moisture dripping down everywhere, but it was a little warmer. We found some not too wet weeds and leaves and put them down on the floor, and that helped some. Then Alexei produced a flint and tinder box and prepared to make a fire. "What do you think you're doing!" hissed the mother of the baby, a woman from our village named Khroska. "You're not going to make a fire? Why don't you just stand outside the cave and shout to the Germans?"

Alexei decided to be patient. "The brush in front of the cave will block any light. The smoke is the thing to be concerned about, but, even if it were daylight, they couldn't see it, because of the fog. It's perfectly safe, and we need to dry our footgear as quickly as possible." And without waiting for a reply, he scratched sparks into the little pile of charred cornstalk material, protecting it with cupped hands and blowing gently on it. Watching him, I marveled. How could he, at twelve, only a year older than I was, know so much more than me?

As we crowded around the little fire at the cave's mouth, a discussion developed as to why the villages in the area were being evacuated and where the convoy was going. For once, Alexei did not have the answer. Neither did anyone else; all we knew was that we had heard we were being taken to an "assembly point"—assembly for what?

We fell asleep almost immediately, and the next day, which brought more rain and three more convoys, there was too much activity on the road to risk leaving the cave. But when most of the afternoon and early evening had passed without further traffic, mother made an announcement: she was going back for Babunia, and to bring food. There was a clamor of protest, but her mind was made up; there was no telling how long they might have to stay in that cave—it might even be until the Russians drove the Germans out of the Dnieper bend—and we couldn't very well eat wet leaves. The issue was settled when Khroska and another woman from our village said that they were going with her. Khroska knew her baby could not survive much longer without proper nourishment.

The road was more difficult than ever that evening, and they were not surprised that there was no one on it. When they finally reached the village, there was no movement there, either; the Germans had dug in along the high west bank of the Dnieper, which was ideal for defense, and few were in the village itself.

The three women leaned against the wall of an old barn at the edge of the village and rested, agreeing to meet back there in about a quarter of an hour. Being careful to stay out of sight as much as possible, mother made her way to the back of our house and to the keep-hole. The wooden cover was gone, and Babunia was not there. Neither was there any food; the Germans had obviously taken everything they needed and destroyed the rest, smashing the sauerkraut barrels and the clay pots containing beets and tomatoes.

Nor was Babunia in the house, both doors and all the furniture of which had been removed by the Germans for kindling. Standing in the middle of what was once our home and conscious that time was passing quickly, mother became frantic; she had no idea where to look next. Out of the corner of her eye, she noticed a movement in the road. It was our cat, which we had also left behind.

The cat looked straight at mother, then licked some mud off of his coat and walked across the road and into the cow shelter next to a house that had been flattened by shell-fire. On intuition, mother checked the road in both directions, then quickly followed.

Babunia was there, lying huddled up in the darkest corner. When she saw mother, she gave a feeble cry of joy, despite mother's signal to her to keep still. Mother went over to her and took her in her arms, and found that she was shivering and at the same time burning with fever.

"I knew you'd come back for me," Babunia said. "When the Germans were ransacking the place, some time after they'd taken you away, they found me in the keep-hole and made me get out so they could get our food. I guess they thought I wasn't worth wasting a bullet on." She laughed and began to cough. When she could get her breath, she went on. "While they were busy in the hole, I slipped over here, where they'd already been. But I got soaked in the rain, and there was no way to get dry or keep warm. So I just prayed." She smiled. "But I'm afraid you're going to have to carry me, because I'm too weak to move."

For a long time, mother said nothing and could not bring herself to look at her.

"Maria? What is it? Why aren't you—"

"Because I can't carry you, that's why! The mud is so bad, I barely made it here myself. In a way, I'm almost glad the Germans took all our food, because I don't think I could carry even a little of it all the way back to that cave." There was another silence.

"But you *can't* leave me again! Maria, please don't leave me here to die!" and she began to weep.

"Then you tell me, Babunia: what *can* I do? I have two boys and a little girl in a cave back there. I can't possibly carry you. Even if you could walk now, in your condition you'd never make it. To be honest, I don't know how far you'd get, if you were perfectly well." And *she* began to cry. "So tell me," she sobbed, "what should I do?"

Babunia took a deep breath. "Go to them," she said and smiled. "God will take care of me." And then she added, "He will take care of you, too. Each one of you."

Mother kissed her and heaped as much dry straw around her as she could find, then kissed her again and left. She hurried to the old barn, aware that she was late and that every minute they stayed in the village increased their chances of getting caught. Yet at the barn there was only the third woman, very worried; Khroska was nowhere to be seen. They waited as long as they dared and headed back to the cave.

Suddenly in the night they heard a woman screaming, "No! No! Please don't take me from my baby! You've got to let me go to my baby!" Fear clutched their hearts—the voice, now fading in the distance, was Khroska's.

Later that night, there was a commotion outside the cave, and in came Khroska with a German officer and several soldiers. "I had to tell them!" she shouted. "They were going to take me to the assembly point! I just couldn't leave my baby!" No one answered her, as the Germans searched the back of the cave, to make sure they had all of us. The next morning, they made a sweep of the entire valley and rounded up dozens of others hiding in other caves, and marched us off to the assembly point, in the town of Marievka.

It would be many years before I fully understood what was taking place at Marievka and other assembly points throughout the Ukraine, and what lay behind the formation of the convoys themselves.

What had set it all in motion, of course, was the rapid deterioration of the Germans' strategic position. By the beginning of October, 1943, the Germans had been in retreat for ten straight weeks without a let-up. To be sure, they had given ground stubbornly, as adept at defense as they were at offense, often holding out against odds of more than six to one, and never allowing a withdrawal to turn into a rout.

But they were very close to the end of their endurance. Too many months of unrelieved combat, too many casualties, too many consecutive defeats without a single victory, too many divisions operating at a third or a quarter of their commissioned strength—mistakes were beginning to happen and nerves beginning to go, professional poise was cracking, and individuals, officers and men, were beginning to think of themselves *as* individuals rather than as parts of units. Unless the Germans were able to buy time—specifically the six-month breathing space between the beginning of the fall rain and the end of the spring thaw that only a stabilized winter front could provide—there was no telling what might happen.

In the north and center, German forces had already been permitted to pull back from Leningrad and Moscow the year before, but in the south, where the great advances of '42 had been made, Hitler was adamant about not yielding another millimeter. He refused permission for a withdrawal from the Crimea, still referring to it in memoranda as "the gateway to the Caucasus," (as if Germany would ever again be able to mount a summer offensive).

As a result, General Mannstein, architect of the *blitzkriegs* that changed the face of modern warfare, was prohibited from simply fortifying the Dnieper River all the way to its mouth, and instead had to extend his line due south from around Zaporozhye, to cover the rear and protect the supply corridor of the troops holding the Crimea. What was worse, he desperately needed those troops, both as reserves and to deepen defenses on the winter line enough to give it a real chance of stabilizing. For when the Dnieper froze in December, it would freeze solid enough to support a column of the heaviest Russian tanks, anywhere they chose to cross.

And there was something else on Mannstein's mind: under most conditions, the German soldier, by training and nature, was as effective as any soldier on earth. But in two years the Germans had scarcely begun to adapt to the unbelievable extremes of the Russian winter, which the Russians

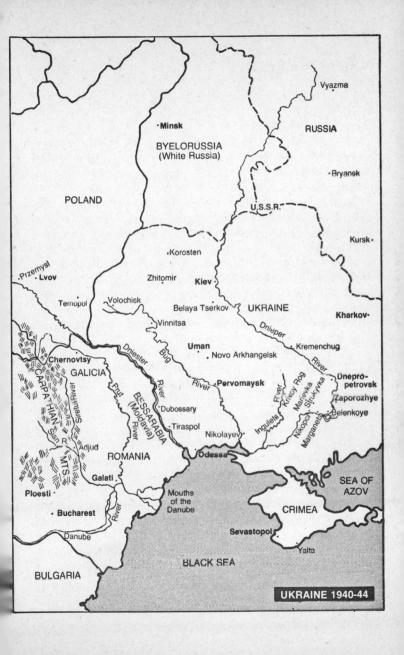

themselves took as a matter of course. Also, in civilian life, the Russians had grown so used to functioning on little or no food that they could go for any number of days without rations if necessary, something which the Germans had great difficulty doing. And they knew how to dress for extreme low temperatures, how to detect the first signs of frostbite, how to husband their body warmth, how to guard against snow-blindness, how to build shelters in deep snow—all things the Germans simply could not assimilate that quickly. In short, they were superb, deep-winter combat troops, which the Germans weren't.

All this Mannstein knew, as he pleaded with Hitler as often as he dared for the use of the Crimean troops. But the Fuhrer's will was set. And so, through the late summer, as the front-line troops slowly gave ground, defensive positions were being prepared behind them, along the west bank of the Dnieper, for them to fall back into—and hold until April, with little depth.

They were too thin. Already by mid-September, Russian generals Vatutin and Koniev had forced bridgeheads across the Dnieper, though for the moment they had been contained. But while German attention was focused on Vatutin's threat to Kiev, Koniev broke out of his bridgehead at Kremenchug, and in the first two days of October had stormed half-way across the Dnieper bend. Maneuvering desperately, Mannstein succeeded in checking the advance just before the rains came two weeks early, but the effort cost him all his reserves. Any attack now. anywhere along the 700-kilometer line. . . .

In the meantime, in the heart of the Fatherland, every able-bodied (and not so able-bodied) German from fifteen to forty-five had been pressed into service to replace the staggering and totally unforeseen losses on the eastern front. Only one reservoir of manpower remained: the workers in the factories that kept the German war machine in operation. Women, to be sure, filled in on the assembly-line, though never to the extent that they did in the Allied countries. For the Nazis had another solution, one more in harmony with—and in fact, a natural projection of—their basic geopolitical construct: slave labor.

Almost overnight, the Slavic races, which had hitherto been regarded with contempt as demonstrably inferior (for instance, the Germans saw no need to bother feeding or sheltering their Russian prisoners of war), were now seen in a new light, as a valuable resource, to be plundered like any other—Ukrainian wheat, oil from Maikop, or manganese from Nikopol.[1]

As long as the Germans had held the Ukraine, the black-earth farmers were more valuable right where they were, on the land, producing. But now, at the beginning of October, 1943, with the deep penetration of the Russians making it obvious to even the most fanatical Nazi that the Dnieper bend was not likely to be held very much longer (let alone through the next summer's growing season), they would no more leave behind such a valuable labor force

---

1. Himmler, in a speech to his SS officers at Posen in Poland, on October 4, 1943, as much as admitted that they had made a mistake in letting so many Russian prisoners starve and freeze to death. "At that time [1941], we did not value the mass of humanity as we value it today, as raw material, as labor. What . . . is now deplorable, by reason of the loss of labor, is that the prisoners died in hundreds of thousands of exhaustion and hunger." (Shirer, p. 954.)

By the end of 1944, three quarters of a million Russian prisoners of war were laboring in German factories and mines, even manning German anti-aircraft batteries, in direct violation of the Hague and Geneva conventions. No Allied prisoners were forced to perform such tasks.

than they would abandon an expensive piece of machinery.

A massive evacuation of that entire region was immediately begun. Upwards of five million civilians were taken from their homes in occupied territories and transported by convoy and cattle-car to labor camps in the heart of the Fatherland. And with the exception of any stray Jewish families that happened to turn up in the net (and which were sent directly to the death camps), the Ukrainian families were separated: the men were sent to work in factories, or to the front lines to dig fortifications (and some were given the opportunity to volunteer to fight); the women, to work on farms or as domestics; the young boys, to be trained as apprentices; and the young girls. . . .

And since a dead slave was of no use to anyone, the word came down: do not execute Slavs for minor infractions. This, however, was not to be taken for a change of heart on the part of the Nazis.[2] Not even with the end in sight and the spectre of inevitable accountability looming ever larger, did they moderate the extremes of their grotesque behavior. On the contrary, it seemed that the more impossible it became for them to avoid reality, the more determined they were to do just that.

And here was the fundamental behavioral difference between the Nazis and the Communists: in their private thinking, the Communists were absolute realists, whatever one might deduce from their public statements. The Nazis,

---

2. In his speech of October 4, Himmler went on to say, "What happens to a Russian, to a Czech, does not interest me in the slightest. . . . Whether nations live in prosperity or starve to death like cattle interests me only insofar as we need them as slaves to our *Kultur*. . . . Whether 10,000 Russian females fall down from exhaustion while building an anti-tank ditch interests me only insofar as the anti-tank ditch for Germany is finished. . . ."

on the other hand, were idealists, however weird and distorted their ideal might have been, and they willed themselves to believe categorically in their ideology. It was by sheer willpower that they could blind themselves to the monstrous side-effects of their self-deification—racial genocide, enslavement on a scale that had not been seen since Roman times, and a hardening of the heart to the degree that humane response was regarded as perversion (a sign of weakness, that one was unfit to rule), and perversion was accepted as the norm.

Strength of will was one thing they had in abundance, and Nietzsche, the spiritual father of National Socialism, had made it clear that this strength of will was the measure of how much a man deserved to be ranked among the *Ubermenschen,* the "overmen," the race of man-gods whose destiny it was to rule the world.[3] And that is precisely what the Nazis had set out to do: fulfill their manifest destiny.

But just as power tends to corrupt, so corruption holds within itself the seeds of its own destruction. Hitler was no freak aberration; he was the archetypal end-product of the system which created him, even as he participated in its creation. The seeds of madness were already there; absolute power merely removed all checks and restraints that would hinder it from coming to full flower. And so Hitler, against all logic and all advice, turned on the one adversary on the planet who was as dark and as mad as he was, and

---

3. According to Nietzsche, all human behavior could be reduced to one basic drive: the will to power. Christianity was the great obstacle to Nietzsche, for it claimed that such power belonged only to God. "Christianity," he said, "has waged deadly war against this higher type of man . . . has sided with all that is weak and base, with all failures. . . . The God on the cross is a curse on life, a pointer to seek redemption from it. . . ." (*The Will to Power,* note # 1052)

they proceeded to rend and tear at one another in a battle to the death. One readily commiserates with those who were caught in the middle like apples in the jaws of a cider press. But when one ponders what might have happened had the Russo-German non-aggression pact remained intact, one sees more clearly than ever the hand that shapes the course of human events, global as well as personal, in response to prayer.

But it would be many years before such things would become clear to me. On that miserable morning in early October, 1943, as I was trudging through the mud and freezing rain, all I knew was that I was still alive. I also knew that I didn't much care. That morning, I just had to lay down and rest, and I wandered off the road and leaned over to do just that, when a whip sang out and bit the seat of my pants. *"Ow!"* I hollered, furious, whirling around, "who the—oh, *no!* It can't be!"

six

My father stood up in the front of a wagon, grinning hugely. A rush of questions tumbled into my mind, even as I called to Alexei and Mother. . . . Where had he come from? How did he ever find us? Where did he get the wagon? But there was no opportunity to ask anything until several hours later, when the German guards halted the convoy so that they could eat their lunch. Even then, father would not permit questions, but merely told us what he felt we needed to know (which was substantially less than our own estimate).

He had not left the Ukraine after all, but had been in a city to the west (which city or doing what, he didn't say). As conditions under the Germans grew steadily worse, his conscience had apparently begun to bother him (which was something new for father, who had never given any indication that he possessed one). So when the directive came out, about rounding up all able-bodied citizens and shipping them back to Germany, he headed immediately for our village ("acquiring" the wagon and horses on the way), only to find that it had already been evacuated. After that, it was a matter of locating the convoy we were in before it reached the separation point ("assembly point") at Marievka.

"This convoy was supposed to get there before dark," he concluded, "but in this mud, it will be more like midnight. When we get there, I have made an arrangement with a man I can trust—"

Just then, a German officer signaled a sergeant who blew his whistle. "All right, get up and get moving!" And everyone wearily began getting to their feet and stumbling back into the mire that was once a road.

All that afternoon Alexei and I labored behind the wagon. There was no riding now; the mud was so deep that we had to pull the spokes of the wheels around by hand and remove great masses of clotted mud as it came up between them. As much as I speculated on what father's arrangement might be, I could come up with nothing, except that, because it was a scheme of father's, it would probably work. As much as I hated him, I had to admit that.

Just before dark, I leaned against the back of the wagon for a moment to catch my breath, and wiped my brow on the still unmuddied sleeve at the crook of my elbow, when I glanced up and thought I recognized the woman in the wagon behind ours. Looking closer, I saw that it was indeed Khroska, and my heart filled with foreboding. She was eyeing us strangely, and the thought flashed through my mind that she had somehow divined father's arrangement. Would she betray us again? That, of course, made no sense at all, but I could not shake the feeling of dread.

As father had predicted, we did not reach Marievka until late that night, though it was only ten kilometers from where we had stopped at noon. Marievka was a real *town*, with two-story houses lining the streets, each with its own courtyard in front and surrounded by a tall fence and gate. At the outskirts of town, everything was in unbelievable chaos. Convoys were arriving from all directions, people were milling everywhere, and for once the German passion for control seemed to have lapsed. In the heavy mist, the only illumination came from a bank of floodlights that the Germans had erected, and they were trying to bring some kind of order into the funneling process as people were directed down the main street toward the checkpoint at the center of town. Guards were shouting commands in German that no one could understand, children and parents were getting separated and screaming for one another, horses were neighing—and my father was grinning from ear to ear.

At least the roads were dry enough here that we could ride instead of push, I thought, as our wagon started down the main street. I could not take my eyes off the procession behind and beside us. The heads of the people in the street seemed to take on an eerie glow in the mist, outlined as they were by the floodlights behind them. I shuddered—they were like the apparitions that the girl who liked to frighten us used to describe. And there was such an air of defeat about them, heads bent, passing by silently, as if they had been shambling along that way since the beginning of time and would be when time came to an end. There was something so lost about them, so forlorn, that it made me want to cry, even wail, without knowing why. Their procession also reminded me of something—something important—but I couldn't remember what.

Our wagon was half-way down the third block, when I heard three quick whistles from off to our right. Instantly my father wheeled the horses to the right, and it looked like we were about to run smack into the courtyard wall next to us, when suddenly a gate opened directly in front of us, and we passed through. Two other wagons followed right behind ours, and just as quickly, the gate was shut again. Alexei and I gaped at each other, speechless.

Father jumped down from the wagon and conferred briefly with the other two drivers, then got back up and told us what was happening. "We're safe here for the moment, but we'll have to be gone before dawn. Well, Maria," he said, turning to mother, "What have you decided?" I looked at mother and was surprised to see tears in her eyes.

"I can't leave the Dneiper bend as long as there's a chance that Babunia might be alive," she said in a whisper.

My father swore then, equally quietly. "But you can't go back to the village," he said, as if reasoning with a slow child. "The Germans are there, and they'll just pack you up and ship you off." And he waited.

Mother said nothing, and the tears brimmed over.

"Listen!" My father hissed, "you're throwing away everything for a corpse! That old woman could not have lasted two days, let alone five! She was sick, with no food and no way of getting dry or keeping warm!" He clenched his fist, and I started to move to try to protect her, but he hit the wagon, instead. Something had changed in my father.

"All right," he snapped, "where *do* you want to go, Maria? I will take you there, all of you. And then I will wash my hands of you. Forever!"

My mother thought a moment before answering. "I have family in Strukyvka, an aunt who has a large house. Strukyvka is not that far from our village, and—"

"Enough!" my father said, and leaped back down to tell the other drivers of his decision. While they talked, I looked at the other two wagons for the first time. In the dark it was hard to see anything clearly, but I thought I recognized a form in the wagon next to ours—yes, it was Khroska! So she *was* in on the arrangement! That was why she had looked at us so strangely. I wondered if my father knew about the betrayal at the cave.

"We'll go out the back way, as soon as it's safe," my father said, returning to the wagon. "Vladimir has heard that Strukyvka has not been evacuated yet, and may not be at all. He is going to leave Khroska and her baby at your aunt's, then he's coming with me." Catching the look on my face, he added menacingly, "I have said that it's all right, and it had better be!"

By avoiding the main roads and traveling mostly on field-paths, we reached Strukyvka late the following after-noon. My great-aunt did have a large house all right, large enough that the Germans had requisitioned it and turned it into a field hospital for officers. My great-aunt was given the use of one room in her home, a little square storage room, the width of two arm-spans. With our arrival, there were a total of four displaced families that had to use that space. We were sixteen in all, so that we had to sleep in shifts; there wasn't enough room for us all to lie down at the same time.

Being cheek to elbow with a bunch of strangers was more than my father could stand, even for one night. Though he was dead-tired, he made ready to depart.

"Where will you go?" mother asked him softly.

"I don't know—as far from this *groznaya* war as I can get!" And with that he whipped up the horses and drove out of our lives again.

We had been at the hospital six days, with mother helping the under-staffed nurses with the wounded, when she felt it was time to go for Babunia. She had gotten close to a German woman named Freida who was acting as interpreter, and who had some authority in the hospital. This woman not only took her to division headquarters and obtained permission for her to leave and a safe conduct pass, she offered to accompany mother, in case they ran into any soldiers.

Early on the morning of October 15, mother and the interpreter Freida borrowed a stretcher, a wagon and two horses and set off for our village. It was beginning to freeze at night now, so the roads were in better shape, and they were able to make it to the village in a few hours, time which passed quickly as mother told Freida about Babunia. Leaving the horses and wagon in a thick stand of trees outside the village, so as not to make any noise (for they could not be certain who was occupying the village), they took the stretcher and made their way to the cow shelter where mother had left Babunia, ten days before.

It took a moment for their eyes to adjust to the darkness. There was a mound over in the corner, where Babunia had been. "Babunia?" mother called softly. But there was no movement. Fearing the worst, it was all mother could do to make herself draw near. She moved some of the straw and gasped: Babunia's body was still there, but it was covered with vermin, many as big as mother's little toe, she later told us. And they were feeding on Babunia, even as she watched, horrified. A wave of dizziness and nausea came over her, at the same time she smelled the stench of putrefying flesh, and she had to go back outside. She sagged against the side of the doorway, her eyes closed and tears started to form in them, when Freida called, "Maria! Come quickly!"

"What is it?" she cried, hurrying back inside. The interpreter did not reply. Instead, she pointed to a vein on the side of Babunia's forehead. Her skin, already wizened with age, was stretched even tighter with starvation. The vein stood out in stark relief, and there, on its surface, was the slightest visible movement.

"She's alive," mother breathed. "Dear God in heaven, she's *alive!*" She ran to the door to get the stretcher, and when she came back, Freida cautioned her to lift Babunia as gently as possible, for whatever life was left must be hanging by a thread. They eased her onto the stretcher, and gingerly lifted her and started carrying her to the wagon. Mother was stunned at how little she weighed; her half of the stretcher couldn't have weighed more than thirty kilos.

They settled her into the back of the wagon, making her as comfortable as possible, though she had yet to regain consciousness. Once underway, mother gave vent to her joy. "I had a feeling she was going to be all right! I can't describe it, except sometimes I seem to know things," she paused and breathed in the crisp October air, as if smelling it for the first time. "Babunia was—is—that way, too. Also, I think God loved her too much, to let her die that way. They were very close," she added, as if speaking of two old friends. Then she laughed and looked up at the clear, deep blue sky. "You and I were close that way once, too, God. We will be again. Thank you for saving Babunia."

When they arrived at the field hospital, the head nurse took one look at what was on the stretcher and refused to let Babunia be brought in. Though Freida argued with her, the nurse prevailed, insisting that it would be an insult to the wounded officers, and besides, hygienically it was out of the question. She did, however, provide the precious sulfa medication that would kill infection, as well as dressings, vitamins, rubbing alcohol, sponges, a basin and other supplies that they would need, and mother and Freida took Babunia to the house of a cousin of mother's aunt. In the Ukraine, when everything else was gone, one could almost always count on family.

This house, too, was overcrowded, but compassion proved stronger than infestation and putrefaction, and they made a whole room available to Babunia. Mother and

Freida put Babunia's stretcher on the floor and kneeling beside it, began to remove the filthy rags that clung to her body, and kill the vermin with a strong antiseptic solution. They moved very slowly, so as not to unnecessarily disturb the already festering flesh. When that was done, they bathed her all over, and probed the deeper wounds to remove any larvae. "Just pray we don't find gangrene," Freida said, and mother nodded.

All the while, Babunia lay unconscious, almost as if she was merely sleeping. There was such a sense of peace about her that it seemed to flow into mother and Freida, without their even being aware of it. Finally, as they were wrapping bandages around the running sores, Freida had to comment: "Your grandmother—she must have been a very special person."

"She is," mother smiled.

"I—I don't believe in God," Freida stammered, "but when I was little, I used to wonder if there were such things as saints." She swallowed and looked away. "I think I've just met one." And she left quickly to change the soapy water in the basin. Mother bowed her head and prayed. When she looked up, there seemed to be the faintest suggestion of a smile on Babunia's lips. And somehow mother knew that she had passed from unconsciousness into sleep.

seven

Alexei and I were not allowed to see Babunia until the
following morning. There was sun streaming in the window
of the room in which she slept, and while mother had
cautioned us to keep our voices down when we looked in on
her, we were not prepared for how much weight she had
lost, particularly when she'd had so little to begin with.

"Mother! What's the matter with her?" I blurted out,
forgetting to whisper. "Her head looks like a—a skull! Are
you sure she's alive?"

And at that, the smile on the face on the white sheet grew
a little larger, and the blue eyes fluttered open. "I'm alive,
Vasya," she rasped, "now be still, so an old woman can get
some rest." And she closed her eyes again.

"Babunia!" I shouted and would have bounded to her
side, except that mother was just able to catch my arm.
"Babunia!" I called again, "It's like the time I drowned, only

now it's the other way around, remember?" And she nodded slightly, without opening her eyes.

In the days that followed, Babunia grew steadily stronger. Mother was needed at the hospital, and Alexei was interested in the German artillery battery nearby, so I wound up spending as much time with her as I could, whenever the Germans would allow us to walk the streets. Babunia never did fully regain the weight she had lost, and from that time on her skin had a translucent quality. Where before, she had looked younger than her seventy-three years, now she looked much older, but there was none of the infirmity that often accompanies extreme old age.

She was changed, though, in other ways, and the one that was most obvious was how at peace she was. She had been peaceful before, to be sure, but now there was a volume to it—like a lake that had suddenly had a hundred fathoms added to its depth; the surface looked the same, but the lake was different. Just *being with* Babunia seemed to dissolve a person's anxieties, even if they were never mentioned by him or Babunia. I didn't understand it, but it was like a drink I could never get enough of.

Babunia spoke even less now than she had before, and she had never been given to unnecessary conversation. On the other hand, when she did speak, there was a depth and wisdom there that may have been there before, but I had never noticed. Also, what she had to say was more often about God and Jesus Christ, and it was not because of the absence of the Communists and the indifference of the Germans. When she spoke of Jesus, she called Him that, not "Christ" or "the Lord," and she spoke His name as if she had just been walking with Him in a garden.

Now, all of the stories she told me were of Him, and while sometimes it was hard to believe that He had actually lived and was, in fact, still alive, in the air, even so, listening to that, for not even Babunia was as old as some of the tallest fir trees across the Dnieper from where we lived.

God had put the star in the sky over a little town a long way to the south of us called Bethlehem, because His Son was going to be born there, just as He had said in His book that He would, and I thought back to the beautiful black leather book Babunia had told us a story from, once a long time before.

When the story ended, I was really sad, partly because I wanted it to go on, and partly because I was afraid that I liked it even more than the one about the Land of Milk and Honey which was my very favorite, and to which I wanted to remain loyal. But when we finally went to sleep that night, I closed my eyes and imagined that Alexei and I were among those shepherds, and I felt so good that I cried.

Early the following morning, Christmas Day, a tremendous explosion shook the hospital. The Russians had begun shelling Strukyvka, and were laying down such a barrage that the Germans feared they were about to open a winter offensive. Everyone was very depressed at the hospital, because they had all been hoping that the winter line had stabilized, and that they would not have to retreat again until after the spring thaw.

About noon, Alexei came bounding in. Mother had tried to keep him indoors during the shelling, but he would have none of it; the artillery battery, *his* battery, was returning fire, and he wanted to be there. "Vasili! It's happened!"

"*What's* happened?"

"The Russians are getting ready to attack. Come on outside." And ignoring mother's commands, I pulled on my

those stories made me feel awfully good, like imagining
goodness of the fruit in the Land of Milk and Honey
ning down my throat into my stomach.

On the night of December 24, we celebrated Jesus' b
day, in a way we never had before. Before, when we v
under the Communists, it was called the night of *Dyedma*
Old Man Frost. It was a night where people would com
your door, and if you didn't have some food for them, c
they were older, some vodka, they would play a trick on y
like painting your house black. But on this Christmas E
Babunia arranged a celebration for the three of us, and c
cousin Lydia, whose mother Fenka had appeared one c
and gone away, leaving her with us. Babunia promised
tell us the real meaning of Christmas, through the story
the *real-life* story, she made it clear—of the first Christn
Eve.

Earlier, she had sent Alexei and me out to get a *yalka*,
little fir tree, and that evening, after a meal made from fo
the German nurses had given mother, and which feature
paska, the creamy-smooth, fluffy egg-bread normally r
served for Easter, she produced a special suprise for us. Sl
had us close our eyes, and when we opened them sl
brought out the yalka with four lighted little candles on
and four sugar-cookies, one for each of us! Happily munc
ing on our cookies, our stomachs full for the first time
almost three months, we gathered around Babunia to he
the story and gaze at the flickering candles on the little tree

It was a wonderful story, of a magic star that had lit up t
night like no other star had ever done before it. And
happened long ago, so long ago, Babunia said, that if o
little yalka were alive then, it would have to grow up to b
great tree, and, just before it died, throw off a pine-co
which would become a yalka itself and grow up, and tl
would have to happen twenty times. Our eyes grew wide

coat and valenki and ran out after him. The field hospital was actually in front of the German lines by several hundred meters, well into the two-kilometer no-man's-land. The Russians knew that it was a hospital and left it pretty much alone, so that outside, on top of the flat snow behind us, we could clearly see the Germans running around their big guns, and in front of us, much farther away, we could barely make out the Russians doing the same thing. It was an eerie feeling, as if the whole thing were a dream. When the Germans fired, we could even see the shells passing overhead and could watch where they landed, though most of them exploded in the air, just before they hit the ground.

After watching awhile and seeing nothing unusual happening and beginning to get cold, I asked Alexei, "What makes you so sure the Russians are going to attack? There's a lot more shooting, but otherwise they're not doing anything that they haven't been doing for the past two weeks."

"Well," Alexei replied somewhat lamely, "over at the battery, a Ukrainian who understands German told me that he had heard the entire German front was collapsing."

I said nothing but turned and went back in the house; we'd heard that kind of thing before.[1] And that night at

---

1. Four weeks before, to be exact. As Mannstein had feared, in using all his reserves to stop Koniev's thrust from Kremenchug, he had dangerously weakened the entire southern line. So when the Russians' next assault came, an attack in force below the Dnieper bend, he faced an agonizing decision: if he pulled troops out of the line to the north, that was practically giving Kiev to Vatutin on a platter. But not to do so could mean literally sealing the fate of thousands of men still holding the Crimea.

And Mannstein had another problem: an extreme shortage of fuel. In fact, so grave was this shortage throughout the German army that almost all gasoline was reserved for emergency use supper with all the others (we were back on potato soup, with fewer potatoes than ever), when the conversation inevitably turned to what Alexei had heard, everyone was in agreement that it was just a wild rumor. Already the shelling had mostly died away, and people convinced themselves that it was just the Communists spoiling Christmas.

Everyone that is, except mother, who said nothing but had a worried look on her face. When I asked her afterwards what the matter was, she said quietly, "I'm afraid that your brother heard the truth, though it may be a week or two away. I don't know why, but I think we're going to be

---

only, with tanks and combat aircraft receiving top priority. As a result, trucks, personnel carriers and staff cars began appearing everywhere with large cylindrical boilers alongside, which would burn wood, one by-product of which was a methane-like gas that gave them some minimal capability, albeit much reduced.

What this meant to Mannstein was that the mobility of even the forces he had was severely curtailed—like playing chess, when your opponent is allowed two moves for every one of yours. In the end, he decided that he had to let the Crimea go, and so the Russians under Malinovsky reached the mouth of the Dnieper by early November.

Simultaneously, Vatutin broke into Kiev and in one week had driven 140 kilometers westward, to the junctions of Zhitomir and Korosten, almost at the Polish border. It was then that the rumors of collapse began to fly up and down the front. But Mannstein was a professional of the old German officer corps and refused to allow himself or any of his staff to be pushed into panic. Improvising brilliantly, he made up a Panzerkorps from the fragments of shattered divisions, and drove the Russians all the way back to Kiev. In fact, had it not been for the critical fuel situation, that counter-attack might even have developed into an all-out offensive, for the Russians had seriously over-extended themselves. What it did do was stabilize the southern sector for another three weeks, though at the expense of most of the emergency fuel reserves

going west again soon, and we had better get ready." She shook her head. "I wish your father were here! He'd know what to do."

I was shocked to hear her say that, after the way he'd treated her, and when I told Alexei about it later, I made the mistake of not keeping my voice down. Of all people, Khroska overheard me and went immediately to my mother. "Listen, Maria, you want Ivan back? Well, I want Vladimir back, too. Just before he left here, Vladimir said something about them maybe going to Nikopol. I think we ought to go there ourselves, and see if we can find them. They left us their wagon and their lame horse, whose leg is healed enough to take us."

If I was shocked before, I was flabbergasted to hear mother agree. Didn't she know the woman was not to be trusted? Apparently not: "I'll see if Freida can arrange for passes for us, and we'll take Alexei and Vasili, to help us in the snow, in case we get stuck." Khroska scowled at this last, because she knew how I felt about her, but she said nothing; without mother's cooperation, there was no chance of getting permission, let alone passes.

The next few days flew by. Alexei reported increased activity in the Russian lines; apparently the only thing that was holding up a move on their part now was a lack of armor—all their available tanks were up north at Kiev. The Germans must have thought an attack was imminent, too, because huge Tiger tanks began rumbling into Strukyvka and taking up defensive positions.

The night before we were to leave, I was able to go to Babunia, and I poured out my heart to her about how I felt about mother wanting my father back and us having to take Khroska with us, to look for him. As I knelt by her bed, she caressed my hair with her fingers, as she used to when she was telling us a story. She just let me get it all out, and as usual, I started feeling better, almost before I began, knowing that somehow she would make it all right.

And she did, but not in the way I expected. "You *all* need your father now, as you never have before. And so I have been asking God to bring him back to you, though I doubt if you'll find him in Nikopol." She looked at me then, as if trying to decide how much to tell me. "You're a good boy, Vasya. Your brother is quicker than you are, brighter, but he lives in his head. You live in your heart, and your heart is good; as long as you act instinctively, you will do the right thing. Learn to trust your instincts. The head is important, a useful tool, but the heart is where God speaks to you."

She smiled. "So you're going on a trip tomorrow!" she exclaimed, changing the subject. "Do you know what day tomorrow is?" I shook my head. "It's the sixth day of the new year, the day that the Old Church marks as the day when the three magicians came to Bethlehem, to pay homage to the babe. One of them, some say, came from as far away as the eastern shore of Russia, where Vladivostok is now."

"How did they know about the babe?" I asked, hoping to lead her into telling me another story about the baby Jesus.

"They were magicians, weren't they? Magicians know all about the stars and such things. They believe that they can read things in the stars, things about the future. And sometimes God does put a sign in the heavens as a signal that He has done, or is about to do, something special. But when it comes to reading the future in the stars, that's the work of the Evil One. God doesn't have to use stars to tell His children what will happen to them, not when He can speak directly to their hearts." And she waited for me to ask the question that was on my lips.

"But wasn't the birth of Jesus a good thing?"

"Of course! And the bright star was put there by God to

signal it. But the magicians didn't know that it was Jesus who was about to be born. All they knew was that something extremely important was going to happen in the west, and that they should go there. It wasn't until they got to the land of Israel that they heard the ancient prophecies about a King of the Jews being born in Bethlehem, and began to figure out what was happening. And of course the star which they were following was right over Bethlehem."

"What did they do when they got there," I interrupted, anxious to have her get on with what happened.

"Why, they gave the babe presents, and told His mother how important He was," Babunia chuckled. "As if she didn't already know! But *she* didn't tell them how important He *really* was! She was very wise for such a young girl. . . ." And Babunia's voice trailed off, as she nodded her approval.

"Babunia?" I said, not wanting to let it end. "Why was their coming so special?"

"Well, to the Church, it came to stand for the first recognition of Jesus as the Light of the World, not just for the Jews but for everybody. For you and for me. So, in a way, tomorrow stands for that first time that each one of us realizes that God is God." She gave a deep sigh then, and I knew I should be going.

As I got up to leave, she took my hand. "One thing more," she said, no longer smiling, "your instinct is probably right about the woman Khroska. But it will be all right: God will look after you, and I'll be praying for you from the moment you leave until you get back."

I kissed her and put on my coat. "Remember, Vasya," she said, catching my eye, "do whatever your heart says. Don't reason, just obey."

And I promised her I would.

eight

In what seemed like the middle of the night, there was a great commotion in the dark of the packed little room we shared. Khroska was up and bustling about, anxious to get off as early as possible—in snow, Nikopol was a full day's journey; it would be wise to get there before nightfall—and in her own way, she was making sure that we were all awakened, too.

But mother would not be hurried. From time to time the Germans had brought in a wounded Russian, often shot and left behind on a reconnaissance patrol, and for the past two weeks mother had been tending just such a man. On top of severe internal and external injuries he had contracted pneumonia and was now close to death. For all Khroska's impatience, mother would not leave without first dressing his wounds.

The man was not actually Russian, but Georgian—a subtle distinction perhaps, but one not lost on anyone from the

101

Ukraine. He was a sergeant and on the surface, as gruff and hard-bitten as they came. But mother had listened patiently as she daily changed his bandages—he was grudgingly grateful that at least someone in that place spoke his language—and gradually he had begun to soften. He told her about his own wife and children, and as he began to suspect that his condition was rapidly worsening, he developed a touching concern for mother and the well-being of her family, taking particular interest in the details of the trip she was about to undertake.

"Don't trust anyone," he advised her, as she sat beside him, saying goodbye. "Keep together and stick with the wagon. And be careful not to overtire the horse; four people is a heavy load, even for a good horse on a dry road." She nodded and smiled at him. "Wait a minute!" he said scolding. "You can't go dressed like that!" And he took the full-length winter field coat that was covering him and held it out to her. "Here, I won't be needing this anymore."

Mother started to protest. "No, take it!" he insisted and broke into a coughing spasm. "Damned Germans would only get it anyway," and he had to stop, consumed by a paroxysm of coughing, that brought a trickle of blood to the corner of his mouth. Embarrassed, he dabbed it away and made a great effort to catch his breath. "Thank you, Maria, for everything," he managed, putting the coat in her lap. "And *Bokh svame*—God go with you." And he turned away, so that she wouldn't see the tears welling up in his eyes. She took his hand in hers and pressed it to her cheek and hurried out into the dark, to the rest of us waiting in the wagon.

Khroska wanted to drive, but mother simply took the reins from her as if it had already been decided, stirred up the horse, and we were off. Ahead of us and to the left, a cloudless night sky was beginning to lighten on the horizon, and beneath the wheels, the hard-packed snow crunched smoothly as the horse settled into a brisk trot. I couldn't help grinning, though Alexei, catching my expression, looked at me like I'd gone slightly mad.

Dawn flooded the sky with ever-brighter color, from red-purple to red-orange to white-gold, and in the opposite direction black changed slowly to a blue so bright and rich that it didn't look real. As the sun rose higher, the snow began to dazzle—thousands of points of light seemed to flash by the spinning wheels of the wagon and wash together behind us. I breathed in the chill morning air, more and more till I thought my chest would burst, then let it out with a whoosh and sat back, feeling a little foolish and not caring a bit.

We were out on the steppes and could see for kilometers. Unending snow stretched away to a flat horizon, like a picture I'd once seen of a tiny boat on a very large ocean. While it was still fairly early in the morning, we saw up ahead the crossroads that would take us to Nikopol. A convoy of wagons, each pulled by a pair of huge German farmhorses and filled with teen-age German soldiers, was crossing in front of us, also heading south for Nikopol. *Reinforcements*—the thought went through my mind, and Alexei nodded, as if he had heard me. If they had to resort to farm wagons, the fuel shortage and the situation ahead was more desperate than we had imagined.

The Germans were in a hurry, and soon the last wagon, a little behind the others, was nonetheless a good kilometer ahead of us and pulling away. I happened to glance to the left, at where the sun had first risen a couple of hours before, just in time to see a lone fighter plane come up over the horizon. It was a Russian Yak-9, flying so low that the Germans in the last wagon did not see him coming. I shouted to Alexei and pointed, and as we watched, the plane lined up on them, taking his time, and held his fire until he was less than 500 meters away.

By now we could hear him, and so could the Germans. The first soldiers were just beginning to leap to the ground, when the plane opened fire and parallel tracks of spurting snow raced towards the wagon. An instant later, they hit with such an impact that the wagon seemed to explode before our eyes, sending men, horses and pieces of wagon flying in all directions. As quickly as it had happened, it was over—dark-uniformed, motionless bodies lay scattered in the snow, one horse still writhing in its traces, a lone figure sinking to his knees and holding his head, staring after the receding plane.

Looking in that direction, to my horror I saw that the plane was no longer going away but was leisurely banking around to the right. "He's coming for us!" I shouted and suddenly had the strongest feeling to stay right where I was, even though Alexei screamed, *"run, run!"* and vaulted out of the wagon, his legs churning even before he hit the ground.

Whether the rest of us were all frozen with fear or what, we just sat or stood there by the wagon, which was now stopped, and watched as the plane aligned itself with us, adjusting its wings slightly for the best possible angle of attack, and came in. Again, he held his fire until he was almost upon us, so close that I could see the flashes at the muzzle of the gun in each wing, as he commenced firing. Again, the parallel, converging tracks streaked towards us over the snow, and I threw my arms in front of my face.

The plane roared overhead, the noise and wind of it shaking the wagon and gradually diminishing. I opened my eyes and squinted at the brightness of the snow. I was still alive! So were the others, and then I looked at the snow to our right. There were the tracks, headed straight for us—but about five meters from us, they divided sharply, going off in forty-five degree angles, passing just in front of the horse and just behind the wagon. *Impossible!*

The pilot must have thought so, too, because he banked hard to the left and came back, so low this time that he looked like he was skimming along on top of the snow. And now, because he *was* so low, he opened fire at a greater distance and just kept pouring it on. And now the bullets, instead of digging in, drove *through* the snow so that, instead of tracks, they made deep ditches, racing towards us.

This time, I forced myself to watch. Just as the ditches were about to cut through us, they swung violently to the left and right, narrowly missing us in front and behind. I kept watching, till I could actually see the pilot's face, even to the red star on the front of his leather flying helmet. Then he roared over, and I ducked, because his propeller was so close. He climbed and banked slightly to look back, started around a third time, then changed direction and went on toward the horizon and over it.

I sat there and stared at the churned-up snow less than a meter in front of the horse, until long after the sound of the plane had died away into silence. And the thought came to me: *God was God.* Vaguely, without really registering, I thought: of course. I must remember to tell Babunia.

Mother was the first to come to her senses, and what she said banished any further thoughts of what had just taken place. "Alexei? Where's Alexei?" And she got down from the wagon and began running back along the road, calling out his name. I jumped down, too, and started after her, when something made me look back towards the wagon. Khroska was frantically doing something with the horse's harness. "Hey!" I yelled back at her, "What are you doing?"

She made no answer but hurried the faster to work the

cold leather straps through the buckles. When I realized what was happening, I started running back as fast as I could, getting to the wagon just as she had gotten the horse loose. "Where do you think you're going?" I gasped, grabbing her arm.

I'll tell you where I'm going!" she lashed back. "I'm taking this horse, and I'm getting out of here, before that plane comes back! Now get out of my way, you little *zaraza!*" And she gave me a shove caught me off balance and sent me tumbling into the snow by the side of the road.

Trying to catch my breath, I watched as she stepped up on one of the shafts and got ready to swing her leg up on the horse. In a moment, she would be gone, and we'd be stranded; I had to do something. "Just like back at the cave, eh, Khroska?" I shouted. "You first, and to hell with the rest of us!"

For an answer, she spat down in my direction, and then her lips slowly spread in a smile that was pure malice. "Goodbye, Vasili. Keep warm." And she swung a leg up on the horse.

But that second's delay was what I needed. Having gathered my feet under me, I sprang forward, and just managed to catch the belt of her coat with one hand as she was going up. Furious, she held onto the horse's mane and reins with one hand and clubbed me in the side of the head with the other. She was a big woman, and the blows hurt and made me dizzy, but instead of letting go, I wrapped the fingers of both hands into the belt; if she went now, she would have to drag me with her.

She caught one of my fingers and bent it back fiercely. I screamed, and at that moment my feet went out from under me. The sudden weight unbalanced her, and she came off the horse and landed on me, knocking out what breath I had left. But I did not let go of the belt.

Now she was clawing at my face with her fingers, thrashing around in the snow and trying to get a good kick at me, all the while shrieking incoherently. Let her make all the noise she wants, I thought as I turned my face away; she'll run out of breath that much sooner. Instinctively I knew that was my only hope, for though I was almost eleven, she was much bigger and stronger than I was.

As soon as I thought I had enough breath, I suddenly let go of her belt and stumbled to my feet. I leaned against the wagon, my chest heaving, and waited for her to get up. As she started to do so, I took a deep breath, ran up and hit her in the face as hard as I could. She had a forehead like iron! My hand tingled, and I couldn't make a fist with it after that, yet the blow didn't seem to bother her a bit; in fact, it only enraged her further.

On her feet now, and too close for me to get out of range, it was her turn to swing with all her might. I saw it coming in time to duck, and the blow sailed over my head, which was doubly fortunate because it tired her far more than anything I could have done. At the same time, crouched over as I was, I put my shoulder into her side like she was a wagon stuck in mud, and over we went.

This time, as I scrambled up, my arms and legs felt like they were already dead, and my lungs were searing. But she got up even more slowly, and we stood there, facing each other and blowing great clouds of vapor in the icy air. For a moment my mind began to wander, and I thought how beautiful the little puffs were that we made. Then I concentrated again on what was happening and wondered if it was ever going to end.

I knew if it didn't soon, it would be all over for me. Mustering whatever strength I had left, I lowered my head and charged her, burying my head deep in her midriff. As I connected, I heard the wind go out of her, and when we went down, she landed on her back, and I landed on her stomach. Neither one of us could move after that. Finally I somehow managed to clamber up on top of her and pin her hands down, just as Alexei did to me when we were rough-housing, and he wanted me to give up.

"Do you give up?" I panted, feeling foolish saying that to a grown-up, but unable to think of anything else. She glared at me, then spat in my face. I stood almost all the way up, then sat down as hard as I could, right on her stomach.

"Hunh!" she blew, and with that the fight went out of her. Her anger, with no place to go, turned to self-pity, and she wept bitterly.

"Get up, Khroska, and come with me!" commanded mother who had just finished putting the horse back in the traces. "Vasili, you take the left side, and we'll take the right; we're going to find Alexei," she declared, grabbing Khroska by the collar and marching her in front of her, into the snow alongside the road.

It wasn't long before I heard a faint cry for help, and, yelling for the others, I followed it—to a three-meter-deep foxhole, filled with soft snow, and my brother. "Hey!" I hollered down to him gleefully, "how'd you ever get down there?"

"I don't know!" he yelled back, obviously failing to see any humor in the situation. "All I do know is, I can't get out! Now will you—"

"Did you try, uh, jumping?" I cut him off, unable to resist teasing.

"Vasili, when I get out of here, I'm going to. . . ."

"In that case, I'd be crazy to help you." And with that I stopped, for Alexei could not stand to have his pride hurt. I took off my belt and reached it down to him. It wasn't quite long enough, but mother came up then and held my legs (after making Khroska sit down in the snow nearby). I hung half-way into the hole myself and was able to reach him. How on earth a foxhole even got out there in the middle of nowhere, I swore I'd never know.

We got Alexei out, and mother filled him in on what had happened, while he was out of sight. I looked at him, hoping he would be proud of me subduing a woman twice my size, but he would not look in my direction and acted as if he hadn't even heard.

When we reached the wagon, mother turned to Khroska. "Get in—no, on the floor in the back. And Alexei, you get back there and watch her. Vasili, you ride up front with me." And so we went back to Strukyvka, each lost in his own thoughts.

An hour or so before we got home, the sun went behind the clouds, and at the same time a wind sprang up, so that it was impossible to keep warm, and we kept an eye on each other's noses and cheeks for tiny white spots, the first telltale sign of frostbite. When we were still a kilometer away, we could see that something had changed during our trip. There were German tanks everywhere, more than we'd ever seen in one place, before. And they were Tigers, their biggest model.

At first I thought they were about to launch a major attack, but then I remembered the fuel shortage. "They must be expecting the Russians to make a big push here, eh, Alexei?" I shouted over my shoulder, and then turned to grin at him, anxious to re-establish the old relationship. But Alexei said nothing, did not even look at me. Something else had changed during our trip.

It was getting dark when we reached the hospital, and Freida was waiting for us, outside. "Listen," she said softly to mother, "tomorrow morning the Wehrmacht is going to evacuate Strukyvka. The Russians are beginning to get tanks now, and Division Headquarters anticipates an attack, as soon as the Reds feel they have enough armor." She paused and then continued, looking away, "therefore, Directive 41 will be carried out: 'all able-bodied civilians in the threatened zone will be transported to Germany, forthwith.' " She turned back. "I'm sorry, Maria, civilians are not supposed to receive any advance warning, but I thought you would want to get as much sleep and warm clothing as you can. And, uh," and now she smiled and whispered, "I have some potatoes for your family, that I'll give you just before you go."

Mother gave her a hug and turned to us. "We'll say goodbye to Babunia now."

"Do we have to leave Babunia?" I said, a large lump forming in my throat. "Why can't we just take her with us?"

"Vasili, you of all people should know why! How long do you think she'd last in this weather? How far do you think she could walk, even if it were in the middle of summer? At least here she'll be safe. When the Germans leave, she can move back with her daughter. And, Vasili, when we get there, you let me tell her, you hear me?" She snapped angrily and started walking. But not before I saw the tears in her own eyes.

As sad as I was about Babunia not being able to come, I was also dying to tell her the events of the day, and as soon as we reached the house of my mother's cousin, I was in the door like a shot and into the room that Babunia was now sharing with four others. She was in bed already, but fortunately the others were out in the main room, around the oven.

"Well?" she said after I'd hugged her; she could see I was brimming over with news.

"Well, first I have to tell you about the plane. Babunia, you would not have believed it!" But as I poured out the details, I was surprised to see that she did believe it, every bit of it, nodding her head from time to time and once murmuring, "God is God." I raced on to the rest, ending just as mother and Alexei came in.

"Then you didn't find Ivan?" she asked, looking up at mother, who shook her head. "Don't worry; he will be here when you need him. I have peace in my heart about that." And she smiled, as if he were already back.

"Unfortunately," mother said, more caustically than she intended, "we have need of him right now! Tonight!"

"What do you mean?" asked Babunia, a trace of dread creeping into her voice.

"Because Freida told me that tomorrow morning, the Germans are going to evacuate the town," mother said flatly. Babunia caught her breath and waited. Neither one spoke, and Alexei and I tried hard to keep from crying.

"You're—not taking me," Babunia said at length, and again there was silence. "Oh, dear God, Maria, you can't leave me behind again! I'm your *family*! You're all I have! Please, please don't leave me!" Now Alexei and I were openly sobbing.

Mother said nothing, but her knuckles, gripping the edge of the bed, whitened. When she had gotten control of herself, she said, "Babunia, it was at least thirty degrees below. And there was a strong wind, too, so you can add twenty degrees to that. Even if we had a wagon, and food and blankets, in your condition you wouldn't last a single day out there," she stopped, to let that truth sink in. "And the thought of stopping somewhere out on the steppes and digging a hole in the snow to bury you. . . ." And then she lost control and began to cry herself. She kissed Babunia and hurried out, holding the back of her hand to her mouth.

Babunia closed her eyes and took a deep breath, then several more. She seemed oblivious to Alexei and me, as if we had left the room, and I began to wonder if maybe we oughtn't to leave. When she opened her eyes again, her former peace had returned. "Listen, boys," she said, reaching out and taking our hands in hers. "You remember when I told you the story about the Land of Milk and Honey?" We nodded, our crying subsiding. "Well, God is going to take you to that land, and not just when you die—though, of course, you'll go there then, to be with Him forever, if you love Him—but now, *in this lifetime*."

We looked at each other, wondering what it meant. "God is going to take you to the Land of Milk and Honey," she said again, and then, raising up in bed, she put her hand on each of our heads and blessed us. After that, she closed her eyes and composed herself for sleep. We each kissed her, and I stood unable to move, gazing down at the fragile form in the bed, at the seamed but tranquil face whose every line I had traced with my finger as a little child sitting on her lap. The tightness was in my throat again, and I knew it was about to begin all over, when Alexei tapped my shoulder and nodded towards the door.

We walked back to the hospital in the darkness, and in silence, save for the crunching of our boots on the freshly fallen snow.

nine

In the middle of that night, I woke up, listening. What was it? Something . . . my ears strained, as if trying to force whatever it was, to happen again, so that it could be identified. Now others were coming awake, too, and listening; I could tell, not by any sound, but by the absence of sound—the wheezes and heavy, even breathing of regular sleep. It was perfectly still. In the pitch darkness of that little room, everyone of us was wide awake. And listening.

Then it came again . . . outside . . . whispering . . . two men . . . *men* (except for Alexei and me and another boy, there was only an old grandfather with us, and those two were already asleep when we'd lain down). Russian words . . . *they were speaking Russian!*

Fear shot through the room like invisible lightning. There was a gasp, and another; in the dark: we were all holding our breath. Had the Russians infiltrated? Were we

113

about to be shot where we lay, as collaborators? The handle on the door slowly turned.

I could hear Lida trying not to cry and someone else whispering prayers. The door creaked a bit as it opened, and now we could hear the whispering voices more clearly. That wasn't Russian they were speaking, it was Ukrainian! And then I recognized the intonations of one of them: "Father!" I whispered loudly, "over here." All at once there was a great exhalation and muffled exclamation, and some-one lit the little oil lamp.

There stood my father and Vladimir, surprised to see everyone wide awake and staring at them. I was so relieved that it wasn't the Russians that for a moment I was happy to see him. But when he held out his arms to Alexei and me, expecting us to run into them, that quickly changed. We got up and dutifully walked over to him and said, "hello."

"Is that the greeting I get? Here I was, sitting a good hundred kilometers west of here, safe and warm, and my wretched conscience starts working me over again—my poor wife and children, no food, no one to look after them, about to be evacuated any day or executed by the Russians—till finally I couldn't stand it any more and had to come back. And this is the thanks I get! Why you—I ought to take the wagon and leave!"

"Wagon? You've got a *wagon*? They're going to evacuate us in the morning—could we possibly take Babunia? She can have my blanket and food, and I'll keep her warm. Oh, father, could we—"

"*Nyet!* She's too old. No flesh on her. She'd freeze like that!" and the snap of his fingers made us wince. "Besides, it would be one more mouth that had to be fed, and we've got enough of those already. She stays." And he inspected a nail in the heel of his boot. "Oh, one more thing," he said, without looking up, "Vladimir and his family will be in their wagon behind us."

"What?" And in a rush I told him what had happened on the road to Nikopol the day before and reminded him of the incident at the cave, not caring who heard. But it seemed like my father was the only one who didn't hear, never once commenting or raising his eyes from the heel of his boot.

When I had finished, father said, "Vladimir is my friend, and that's all there is to it." And now he did look up, to see if I dared answer back. I didn't. "You'd better get some sleep," he concluded. "We'll be leaving in a couple of hours."

For the second morning in a row we made ready to leave before dawn. As we slipped out the door, Freida appeared. She had obviously been waiting, so as not to miss us. She said goodbye to mother and promised to do her best to see that Babunia was safe. Then, looking carefully around her, she passed mother a little sack with potato-sized bulges in it. Mother hugged her, and Freida blinked back tears. "May God protect you," she said, finally.

Behind us, in the second wagon, Khroska spat in disgust at the scene, while I handed Lida and then Lydia up to Alexei. I got in myself then, and the four of us huddled down in back, while father spread a tarpaulin over us to protect us from the wind. Then he joined mother on the front seat, shook out his whip and gave it a terrific *crack,* and the two horses took off with a start.

I lifted a corner of the tarp to watch us leave. There was no dazzling, heart-lifting sunrise this morning, no sense of anticipation in the swift beat of the horses' hooves or the sound of the snow under the wheels. On the contrary, as the color of the sea is a reflection of the sky, a heaviness that matched the leaden overcast above us seemed to settle over the wagon. I stared at the snow-covered town receding in the distance behind us, and at the massive squat turrets of the black Tiger tanks we passed, their long-barreled guns leveled at the town, waiting. . . .

A shudder passed through me, and not from the snow that was beginning to fall. There, by the side of the road, was an ominous foreshadowing of the days ahead: a frozen corpse, half-covered with drifting snow.

Across the white face of the Ukraine, that January of '44, dark dots marked convoys crawling west. Some were made up of only a few wagons or stragglers, picking their way over the vast, snowbound reaches of the steppes, trying to guess at the whereabouts of the road far beneath the surface, when a blizzard had obscured the tracks of those who had gone before.

Other convoys were several hundred strong, but whatever they gained in numbers (and whether it was a gain was questionable), they lost in mobility; invariably the larger convoys moved at the pace of the wagons in the lead, and if these were not handled well, the pace often slowed to a standstill. Moreover, if there were weak wagons in the middle of the column, those ahead would gradually pull away, until there were, in effect, two convoys.

That was why my father had been anxious to get away well ahead of the convoy that would be formed in Strukyvka. The Germans didn't care. Nor did they bother to assign escorts to guard the convoys, for now that *everyone* was being evacuated, it was simply a matter of making sure that the Ukrainians, wherever they were encountered, were kept moving and kept headed in the right direction: west.

The one thing the Germans had to watch for was civilians trying to hole up for the winter. Normally, no Ukrainian in his right mind would be caught out on the open road during winter. Once the last crop was harvested, and the fall rains came, they spent as much time indoors as possible, seldom venturing forth for other than an emergency, which usually entailed scavenging for food or fuel. And never traveling from one town to the next, if they could possibly avoid it. But now an entire people was on the roads, and the Germans made periodic checks of all empty houses to make sure they *stayed* on the roads.

And so the convoys came, and the roads became arteries, as the lifeblood of the Ukraine flowed westward, leaving her face whiter than ever. In the large cities where the Germans established checkpoints, often the men and older boys were separated from their families and returned to the front, to dig, to lift, to carry—and sometimes, if they volunteered, to fight, though the Germans seemed reluctant to trust those whom they had regarded as subhuman enough to put loaded rifles in their hands.

Those who remained were formed into even larger convoys, as the dots streamed together and formed tributaries, which, in turn, flowed into major rivers of humanity. The mouths of these rivers were located in Poland and Romania. There, at railheads far beyond the reach of the most determined Russian aircraft, the cattle-cars waited. . . .

And all the while, the red wolf was circling the grey wolf, sensing weakness, watching for the pulled hamstring, the unprotected flank. It was bigger now and stronger, and it knew the terrain. The grey wolf maneuvered to be always facing its adversary, snarling and slashing at every testing probe, with fangs that could still inflict fearful damage. But it was growing steadily weaker, from lack of food and loss of blood. It was only a matter of time, and the red wolf could afford to be patient a little longer; it had already waited three years. But not too much longer, the scent of blood was in the air, and the prospect of a kill was becoming more of a reality.

As Hitler had directed on the eve of his surprise attack, the eastern war had not been conducted in a "knightly" fashion. Hundreds of thousands of Russian prisoners-of-war had been left to perish, while their French and British counterparts were fed and sheltered. The lesson was not lost on the Russians; their treatment of their German prisoners soon matched that which they had received, and they had the added incentive of vengeance.[1]

It became a war of no quarter. Whenever a German soldier was killed by partisans, the Germans, in obedience to a directive from High Command, rounded up and executed ten civilians in reprisal. To further discourage partisan activity, any civilian suspected of such activity was hanged from the tops of the trees that stuck above the snow and left there, till a woods outside a fair-sized town would be festooned with corpses, slowly turning in the wind.

As for the Russians—the punishment most feared in the German Army was re-assignment to the Eastern Front.

Hunger and cold gave the Basansky family no quarter that winter. There was never enough to eat, and no matter what measures we took, we never could get actually warm, only slightly less cold. The remotest possibility of food was

---

1. Of the 90,000 German prisoners taken at Stalingrad, fewer than 5,000 ever returned home.

foremost in our consciousness: Whenever we passed the carcass of a recently dead horse or cow, we took what meat we could, though there was seldom much to be had; the horses had usually died of starvation themselves, and if they were more than a few days old, the bones would be picked clean by those who had passed by before us. At least we didn't have to worry about the meat having gone bad, not at thirty or forty below. But an unharvested cornfield was our most common source of food. When father spotted the tops of the stalks above the snow, we would stop and all of us but the two little girls would go into the rows, searching for ears that had not gone bad before they froze. If there was time, we would take the kernels off of them and boil them, to make it easier for the little girls, but more often we simply gnawed on the ears as we went.

While food may have been in the forefront of our minds, the cold was something we could never afford to forget. Pushing the wagon through a deep drift, exhaustion came quickly, and the temptation to just sit down for a moment and take a rest was often overwhelming. Just to shut your eyes and relax—it was amazing how quickly the cold could change to warmth, a warm, dark, welcoming sea of night, lapping over the gunwales of one's mind. . . . In that cold you would last maybe fifteen minutes at the most, if you didn't keep moving, and we would pass the bodies of people who had stopped and had frozen in the attitude of their moment's rest.

Others, of course—many others—would simply give up. Their legs would give out, or their stomachs would swell from starvation, or their minds would cease to focus on reality. Or there would simply be one blizzard or even one drift too many. They would just go and lay down, and it was as if they had pulled a blanket over their head.

Whatever the reason, Death did not keep them waiting

long. In that temperature, anyone who wanted to give in to him was quickly obliged. From the positions of the frozen bodies we passed, it was not hard to tell whether he had taken them unawares, and the majority had not been taken by surprise.

But even knowing all this, knowing the tremendous danger in relaxing one's vigil for even a second, more than once I very nearly wandered over the line. The first time was when my father's whip brought me instantly and painfully back to reality, but the closest time was when I was out of his line of vision. I was pushing behind the wagon, while Alexei and mother were at the front wheels, and father was "encouraging" the horses—with earth-shaking curses and the carefully placed tip of the whip. (Babunia had said that at the peak of his fury he would cause even the Devil himself to tremble, and there was no question that those two horses feared him more than any man or thing they had ever known. As a result, we were often able to make progress when no one else in the column could move—all the more reason why father preferred to have the road to himself.)

All at once, the wagon gave a lurch forward, and I found myself spread-eagled in the snow. It was fresh snow, and fluffy—and surprisingly comfortable, once you got down into it. I had been working hard all morning, and the wagon was moving now; there would be no harm in resting, just until Vladimir's wagon came along. I settled in, faintly wondering if this was what it felt like to float on that river in the Land of Milk and Honey. . . . Far away, down inside of me, alarm bells were going off, but already the edges of my consciousness were beginning to unravel.

"Vasili! *Wake up!*" Somebody—mother it was—was slapping my face and shaking me, only it was all happening far away. It didn't really concern me, and I had no desire to go back there, not when I had finally gotten warm and was no longer hungry. "Oh, God, *do* something!"

Suddenly I was being marched back there, like when I was very little, and Babunia had had ahold of me by the ear. I did not want to open my eyes; that would be a commitment to a reality infinitely less pleasant than the one I was in, but I had no choice.

"Oh, thank God!" mother said, looking down at me. She was crying, and she hugged me, then started to get angry with me, and then hugged me again. It turned out that she had gotten a nudge in her heart that something was wrong, and when she called out to me, and I didn't answer, she started back along our tracks and found me. After that, she kept a close check on both Alexei and me.

The collapse of the German front in the Ukraine did not actually come until early March, 1944. On March 4, Zhukov launched an all-out attack from positions west of Vinnitsa along an eighty-kilometer front, his object being to cut the Odessa-Lvov railroad line which was all that was holding the Germans' Ukrainian front together. In two days his forces advanced seventy kilometers and succeeded in taking the railhead at Volochisk on the main line, and three days later they were in Ternapol.

Meanwhile, on his left flank, Koniev, who had originally threatened the Dnieper bend in October, now unleashed a coordinated attack to the south, securing his first objective, the German base of operations at Uman. With this disaster, the entire defensive position in the Ukraine began to crumble. The seeds of panic finally took root in German military soil.

Our first indication of what had happened came when we noticed that we were no longer the only ones headed west. Before, the only Germans we saw going our way were the wounded; most of the Germans we passed were going in the opposite direction, mostly fresh-uniformed boys not much older than we were—replacements for the Eastern Front.

Now it was different. Hollow-eyed, bearded soldiers joined our ranks—and officers, too, and these posed a new threat, for the convoy pace was not fast enough to suit them: they wanted our horses. One day a young lieutenant, missing his officer's cap and covered with mud, held up his hand and ordered us to stop. Father, sizing up the situation, chose not to hear him, instead kept his eyes on the road in front of him, speaking softly to the horses.

"Halt!" the young officer shouted again, furious that his command had been ignored. Then he pointed at one of our horses and at father and issued a stream of orders in German. While I couldn't understand all of it, his meaning was perfectly clear. Again, father made as if he hadn't heard—until the officer unholstered his Luger and pointed it at him, gesturing for him to get down off the wagon.

Now father professed great surprise, as if noticing him for the first time, and hastened to do as he was bid, making signs that he did not understand any German. But the officer suspected (correctly) that he did, and this only infuriated him the more. Something told me that he was about to kill my father, and my one thought was no, he can't do that; that privilege belongs to me!

I leapt down off the wagon and threw myself between him and my father, just as the officer's forefinger was beginning to tighten on the trigger. With his free hand he tried to push me out of the line of fire, but I clung to him, crying and pleading, offering myself in father's place, until after awhile he put his Luger back in its holster. He was still which was why both adversaries had traditionally waited until mid-May at the earliest before initiating any major operations.

But now the mud did not seem to even *slow* the Russians, let alone discourage them from pressing the attack. The Russian soldiers, long frustrated, outmaneuvered, and denied a conclusive victory, were now willing, even happy, to slog all night through the mud and go without food, if it meant closing the gap by even a few more kilometers. As a result, they were overtaking German units in full retreat, often sweeping right by them and leaving them for the second wave. Thousands of Germans were surrendering every day, but the taking of prisoners meant valuable combat soldiers would have to be withdrawn from the advance to act as escorts. More personnel would be tied up with guard duty and processing, and roads vital to supply and communications would be clogged with eastbound captives. And so the word came down: *nyet plenykh*—no prisoners. The red wolf had drawn blood, and the grey wolf could no longer hold him at bay. The time of the kill was close at hand.

In the southern tributary, Germans and Ukrainians were sharing the same nightmare, for the Russians were not bothering to make any distinction as to whether the Ukrainians were on the road out of choice or not. According to the Communists, anyone who did not stay in their village and die fighting the Nazis was clearly a traitor and deserved to be shot on sight. Nor could they be bothered with the fact that most of those on the road were women and children; they were fleeing the Red Army, weren't they? (If they weren't at the beginning of March, they certainly were a few days later.)

The nightmare was a classic in slow-motion terror. As we struggled through the mud, word would reach us that the Russians were only twenty kilometers behind us, or twelve,

shouting, still in a rage, but I knew the worst danger was past. When he felt his honor, and probably that of the Third Reich as well, had been restored, he left, went to the next wagon in line (which unfortunately was not Khroska's) and commandeered one of their horses.

I was grateful that father did not thank me afterwards—that, in fact, his pride did not permit him to make any acknowledgment of the fact that his twelve-year-old son had just saved his life—because I had not done it out of love. When he died, it was going to be by *my* hand, no one else's—in *my* time, under circumstances of *my* choosing.

In any event, from that time on, whenever a German came and wanted one of our horses, I would be the one who would go and plead with him not to take it, crying and carrying on until he left. And it always seemed to work, possibly because a heart hardened enough to take a horse away from another man, was not quite hard enough to deny a sobbing boy. At the same time another possibility presented itself to me—a notion so strange that I immediately dismissed it from my mind—that somewhere Babunia was praying for us.

ten

The thaw came early, that spring of 1944. The ice began to come out of the ground the second week in March, even as the trickle of Germans on the road became a steady stream. The tributary that we evacuees were in swung to the south, where it was fed by Krivoy Rog and Nikopol, and then ran west along the bottom of the Ukraine, about seventy kilometers inland from the Black Sea. As such, it was the farthest from the rapidly disintegrating front and presumably the safest, and thus it was also the preferred route of Germans who had decided that it was time to get "separated from their units."

But no one, we or they, had anticipated the speed with which the Russians would be able to advance. Normally, we would have welcomed the return of axle-deep mud, taking solace in the fact that, as much as it restricted us, it was also impeding them. In fact, it had been impossible to coordinate and supply a major offensive in the mud-season or six. And as much as we would wish that such reports were the wild rumors of alarmists, almost invariably they turned out to be accurate.

Each such report brought with it a wave of frenzy, as it was passed up the column. And a man in the grip of panic, even a seasoned tanker like those at controls of the fleeing Tigers, tends to lose his professional edge. Time after time, we would watch as a German tank would lose patience and accelerate just a bit more than the mud would tolerate. Suddenly, the tracks would break loose and start to clatter and spin, the engine would race, and the tank would slowly settle deeper into the mud, until its tracks were almost out of sight, spewing up huge clods of mud as they turned. There was nothing to do then but bail out: the turret hatch would open, and the last man out would turn and drop a grenade down the hatch behind him and leap off, as a whanging roar would convert their tank into a flaming ruin.

In the early hours before dawn, an even more bizarre sight was occasionally to be seen. The great compensation the Russians had for pressing forward through the entire night was that inevitably they surprised Germans who had quit at one or two AM for just a few hours of sleep, confident that no Russian would be so fanatical as to carry on past midnight.

Thus, at four or five AM, a tank crew would sometimes be seen running out of a farmhouse and down the road in their underwear, with nothing else but the key-ring to their tank dangling from the forefinger of one of them. And these men would then join the ranks of the walking.

It was obvious to father that the only way we were going to stay ahead of the Russians was to go as hard as they were, which meant traveling all night. Our goal was the Ingulets River; once we were across that, there should be an opportunity to rest. And so he drove the horses unmercifully, and us, too, as mother, Alexei, and I spent hour after hour heaving our weight down on the spokes of the wheels as they came around, and clearing the mud from between them as they came back up. At night he allowed one of us to sleep in the back of the wagon, while the other two worked, rotating us to get the most effort possible from us.

Thus we reached the Ingulets just at dusk, barely three hours ahead of the Russians, only to find that our goal, that had kept us going for three days of no food and no sleep, had become our greatest obstacle. Russian aircraft had wiped out the bridge, and below us at the edge of the river, two to three thousand evacuees were stranded, with no way to get across and nowhere else to go. People were milling this way and that, not knowing what else to do, and some with wagons were going farther up and downstream, only to return with the report that *all* the bridges had been taken out. But most of the people were just sitting in despair, hardly bothering to try to find cover, whenever a Russian fighter came in on a strafing run.

I was too beaten, too disappointed to cry. I just sat with the others, while father went down on foot to reconnoitre the situation. When he got back, Vladimir was just arriving. Father called him down, and they had a conference with a third wagon driver whom they had befriended. At length, father climbed back up on the wagon, turned it around and headed back in the direction we had just come from.

"What are you *doing*?" I hollered. "You're heading right towards the Russians!" Father said nothing, but whipped the horses to the quickest pace they could make. I noted that the other two wagons were following us—and that other people, hurrying along towards the bridge, gaped at us in dismay and unbelief as we passed by.

Eventually we came to what was little more than a cow-path crossing the road, and here father turned the wagon left and headed north. But only for a hundred meters or so. Then he stopped, as did the others, and he and Vladimir went back to the road on foot. They returned in a short while with a great bundle of telephone wire, and I remembered seeing a downed pole and wire, near where we'd turned off. We got underway again, and after awhile swung back down to the river's edge and ran by a forest for a couple of kilometers. We made better time now, because no wagons had cut the ground to ribbons, and also because the horses seemed to have gotten a second wind. These horses were amazing, I thought; smaller than normal, and both mares (a red and a black) seemed to have more strength than pairs half again their size. They were perfectly teamed and pulled as one, and while it was true that they lived in mortal fear of my father, yet I felt there was something more about them . . . .

Just then, father reined in and looked across the river, though it was difficult to make out much. Fortunately for us (and unfortunately for those back at the crossing, which was now a good five kilometers downstream from us) there was a full moon. The river was considerably narrower where we were, but that had a disadvantage: the current was that much swifter.

The drivers got down and put their heads together again, and soon were nodding in agreement. Father came back and drove the wagon down to the water's edge. I thought for a moment he might try to ford, but I realized it was too deep, even as he stopped. He had something else in mind, and as usual, I wasn't about to find out what until it actually happened.

The third man produced some tools, and with these, father proceeded to dismantle our wagon. I bit my lip to keep from giving vent to my curiosity and thus giving him the satisfaction of not answering me. I noted that our wagon was the only one with a square bottom and wondered if that had anything to do with it, but dismissed that thought when the other men started taking their wagons apart, too.

I finally gave up trying to figure it out. The three men stuffed bits of cloth in the cracks of our wagon's box, tied one end of the wire to the back of the box and the other to a tree. Then, taking two planks from the side of one of the other wagons, Vladimir and the third man launched the box and got in it, paddling with the boards, while father paid out wire from our end.

The current was taking the men rapidly downstream, and they started paddling faster. If they didn't make it to the other side, before they used up all the wire, they would be swung down against our side of the river and probably capsized. They paddled as fast as they dared, the spray from their splashes shining in the moonlight, and though they were on a diagonal, it looked like they were more than halfway across. Unfortunately, it also looked like they had used up more than half the wire. And sure enough, just a few meters from the far shore, the wire tautened and swung them, helpless, back out into the middle of the river, where the water began to pile up against the back of the box.

Would it fill and sink? On the other hand, if father cut them loose, they might be swept half-way down to the bombed-out crossing and still might swamp. Neither one happened. By moving carefully to the front of the box, they were able to raise the back end, in spite of the pressure from the wire, and they gingerly paddled themselves to the near shore, climbing out as soon as it was shallow enough to do so safely.

They walked the box back upriver to where we were and had another conference. Apparently they had decided to give it one more try. This time father got in and took Vladimir with him. Again they set out, this time paddling furiously from the outset. They were doing better this time, but still the line began to tauten before they quite reached the other side. With that, my father jumped over the side and plunged into the water and out of sight.

But he reappeared as he found his footing, and was able to drag the box ashore. All the others broke into a cheer, and I did, too, before I realized what I was doing. On the other side, they walked the box back upriver, till they were opposite us, and then proceeded to haul in the wire. When they got it taut, there was more than enough to tie half on the front of the box and half on the back, which they did. Then they gave the signal, and the third man hauled the box back over with father in it.

On the first trip back, father took off his wet clothes, wrapped himself in a blanket, and rode back across, leading the two mares who swam alongside. With them on the other side to do the hauling, the transporting could begin in earnest. Back came the box with Vladimir in it, and he and the third man began filling the box with parts from the other wagons. At that moment, three silhouettes in helmets and carrying rifles materialized out of the darkness.

My heart stopped. My father's shoulders sagged, and the life seemed to go out of all of us. So this would be the end. . . .

But, as it turned out, all they wanted was a ride across, which we agreed to, provided that they left us alone. Which they agreed to—the days of *ubermenschen* and *untermenschen* had long since passed. Fear and necessity had made us equals, at least for that night. When they were across, the next load carried one of the wagons disassembled, and the third the other. By the fourth, all three men were on the other side with the horses, and were busy re-assembling the wagons.

That left Alexei and me to haul the empty box back, snubbing the wire around a tree, to keep it from slipping back. That box weighed a ton! After one trip we were exhausted; father could have stood over us with a whip, and we couldn't have budged. And the worst of it was we didn't have the strength left to pull one of the men back to help us.

I was leaning up against the snubbing tree, keeping the wire from slipping back but unable to help Alexei haul in another meter, when I happened to look up, and there in the moonlight stood the biggest horse I had ever seen. I blinked, and with my free hand wiped my eyes. It was still there—no halter, no bridle, and so clean that it looked like it had just been scrubbed down and curried. In fact, with moonlight on its broad back, it seemed almost to glow. Certainly I had not seen its likes in the Ukraine; even the big German farmhorses that had gone by us that day on the way to Nikopol did not come near the size of this one.

I blinked again. It stood so still in the moonlight, almost as if it wasn't really there, that I began to feel my scalp tightening on top of my head—was it an apparition? Full of dread, I forced myself to look again. It was there, perfectly still, its eyes fixed on me, waiting.

Now I *was* scared, no point in not admitting it—but something drew my attention to the big white blaze on its face. No ghost horse would have a mark like that! I began to smile at my foolishness. I called to Alexei to come and hold the snub, and as soon as he did, I walked over to the horse and put my hand up on that white blaze. The horse seemed pleased and nodded his head a couple of times under my touch.

That was the gentlest horse of any size that I had ever met. I led him to the loose end of the wire, fashioned a halter out of it, and put it around his neck. And from that moment on, the horse did our pulling. What's more, we both got up on his back and rode with him back and forth as he went. And as we did so, I grinned in the dark at our good fortune and realized that this was the most fun—the only fun, come to think of it—we'd had since we left Strukyvka.

Someday I would really have to tell all this to Babunia—this "phantom" horse that had appeared just when we needed him so badly, but was so real that his huge barrel body seemed like it would split Alexei and me in half, as we sat astride him. And then the thought came to me that somehow she probably already knew. And that thought made me very happy, happier than I'd been since we'd said goodbye.

When the job was done, we turned our attention to finding a tree near the edge of the water that we could loop the wire around, so that we could pay it out slowly behind us, until it either ran out, or we were far enough across that it was safe to let go. When we found one and looked up, the horse was gone. Just disappeared, which made me really sad, because I had wanted to take him with us. We looked for him and even called, until one of them on the other side yelled across to see what was taking so long.

When we let go of the wire, we were pretty well across; even so, the wagon box pitched, and the next thing I knew, I was in the water. Reaching out blindly, I felt the trailing wire against my arm, grabbed onto it, and completed the crossing in tow. I was so cold when they pulled me out that mother and father both had to take turns rubbing the warmth back into me.

Looking back, we saw the sky growing brighter downstream, as the Russian planes concentrated their bombardment. Despite the nearness of the Russians, father drove the wagon into an old barn and declared a rest for the remainder of that night, and no sooner had he said so than it seemed that all the fatigue of the past few days caught up with us, and we could barely stay awake long enough to lie down in the wagon together under the tarpaulin, while father sat with his back against one of the wheels.

In succeeding days, the nightmare continued unbroken; only the fear was intensified (if that were possible). For in addition to the Russians behind us, Koniev was pressing down from the north *ahead* of us, and Zhukov was driving for Chernovtsy. His intent was to cut the last rail link between the German forces in Poland and those trapped in the southern Ukraine, where all effective resistance had ceased, and everyone had but one thought: to get out. And the tributary that we were in was the only route left.

As in a classic nightmare from which there was no awakening, scenes began to repeat themselves—the officer waving his pistol and trying to take our horses, the tank helplessly churning deeper into the mud, the tank crew walking dejectedly along the road in their underwear—even the faces began to look familiar. And always in this nightmare, the Russians, almost never seen, were nonetheless in close, relentless pursuit, never much more than an hour behind, sometimes barely a few minutes. We couldn't see them (and had no desire to, for that meant that they could see you—in the circle of a machine-gun sight). But we could hear them—their tanks, their trucks, and the almost incessant small-arms fire—as they caught up with those just behind us.

And as before, there was always a river; if we could just keep going till we got across, we could stop and rest. Yet also as before, when we reached it, the hope turned into horror—though each, in its own way, was unique.

When we reached the Bug, just to the north of Nikolayev, the mud was unbelievable. There was a lone pontoon bridge intact, and heavy German equipment had turned the shoreline and approaches to it into a bog. Here, several thousand evacuees sat and watched as German tanks, half-tracks, and other mechanized equipment lined up to wait their turn. And we sat and watched, too, for the Bug was much too wide to attempt another ferry crossing.

For once, father did not seem on top of the situation. He showed no interest in checking things out for himself. Instead, he just sat there on the front seat, hunched slightly forward, his hands drooping between his knees, the reins slack in his grip. I caught a glimpse of mother's face as she looked over at him, and there was far more concern written there than I cared to admit.

"Well, what's the matter?" she asked in a demanding tone I'd never heard her use with father before. "Why aren't we going forward?"

There was no answer.

"Hey, didn't you hear me? I said, why aren't we going across that bridge?"

"What do you think, woman!" he said disgustedly, "Can't you see they're only letting Germans across?" And he turned back to stare at the scene. I couldn't understand it: first mother said something that was just asking for a beating, and then father didn't even get mad.

But mother did not let it rest there. "Hey, Ivan! Have you gone soft? What am I married to, anyway, a *baba*—an old woman?"

And with that, fire blazed in father's eyes, and screaming through clenched teeth, he took her by the hair and slung her off the wagon. Then, he leapt down himself, picked her up again by the hair and started belting her back and forth with his other hand.

Now screaming myself, I jumped down and was about to throw myself on his back, when I noticed a German soldier standing a few meters away his rifle raised, just waiting for a clear shot at my father. Without thinking, I changed directions and placed myself in front of the soldier, pleading with him not to shoot. This so surprised him that he lowered his rifle, and at the same time my father realized what was happening and ordered mother to shut up and get back in the wagon. Then he did so himself, and after making sure that the soldier had changed his mind, so did I.

But my father was still seething. Grabbing up the whip, he lashed the horses, and they started down the incline at a gallop. What happened next was a string of coincidences, the timing of which seemed to take them far beyond the realm of coincidence (though I didn't have time to think about that until much later).

The momentum of the wagon was such that it carried us through mud which had stalled several trucks and staff vehicles, and before we really knew what was happening we were alongside the vehicle that was next in line to go on the bridge. Just then, a Russian fighter appeared out of nowhere and made a strafing run down the beach, loosing a pair of small bombs just as he flashed over the bridge. He missed, of course—he should have released forty or fifty meters sooner—but the combined effect sent the bridgemaster and guards scurrying for cover.

By the time they got back to their posts, our wagon was already on the bridge, followed by a half-track and two motorcycle couriers. When the bridgemaster saw what we had done, he was so mad, I half-expected him to hit the man next to him just to have someone to hit. For it was too late to have everyone behind us back up, and if he shot us, they'd still have the problem of the wagon and horses.

As we reached the high ground on the far side, another plane came down the river, and this one's release was perfectly timed. Twin geysers went up right alongside the bridge, blowing trucks and pontoons high into the air. Even as we were watching, Russian tanks crested the hill on the side we had just left and started down the slope towards the river, guns and cannons blazing, turning the shore into a slaughterhouse.

After the Bug came several smaller rivers and then the Dniester, the last major river in the Ukraine. As always, it was going to be close; the Russians already held Dubossary on the Dneister, barely sixty kilometers to the north of us, and they were closing so fast behind us, going into the city of Tiraspol, that our only hope was that the prospect of looting would slow them down.

It did, but when we got to the river that night, pandemonium reigned. Again, there was a solitary pontoon bridge, but this time there was no orderly file, nothing but a huge mob of soldiers and evacuees, fighting one another to be next on the bridge and so covered with mud it was no longer possible to distinguish them. It made me shudder just to look at it, though I couldn't see much, except by the glow cast by fires in the city behind us. The mud was so completely churned up that it was thigh-deep and impassable to anything but foot traffic, and even that was difficult. As we watched, planes came over and dropped a series of parachute flares, and as these floated slowly down, covering everything with their icy white light, other planes came and bombed and strafed.

I couldn't bear to watch; people wanted to run when the planes came, but they didn't dare lose their proximity to the bridge, which was miraculously still intact. So the vast hoard at the head of the bridge stayed packed together, and the planes came back and back again.

"Well, Ivan," mother said caustically, "are you going to sit there all night?"

No answer.

"Don't tell me your spine has turned to jelly *again*?"

"*Arrgghh*!" Only this time, he took it out on the horses, standing up in the wagon, flaying them with the whip, and hurling curses down upon them that would make demons in Hell quake. And those horses, out of terror or whatever, pulled as they had never pulled before. Our wagon went where no wagon had passed for hours, and soon we were at the head of the bridge, with father screaming like a madman and whipping people out of his way.

Then we were on the bridge, but still he didn't stop, yelling and laying about him with the whip, to the left and the right, with such fury that people actually began moving out of his way, even on the bridge. And now he re-doubled his efforts, reaching the whip back and hurling it out over the horses—and laughing now, exulting as we moved ahead faster on the bridge. Looking up at him, as he stood up in the front of the wagon, his back illuminated by the light from the blazing city behind us, I shuddered to hear the sound of that laughter. For it indeed sounded like it came from the very pit of Hell.

And then we were across! And we fairly galloped up the embankment on the far side, not stopping till we came to a stand of trees well away from the river. The *last* river! We had made it! The horses stood trembling violently, covered with lather, and then my father sank down on the seat, suddenly exhausted—not just from the final, supreme effort, but from all the weeks of all-out efforts. He turned to see if we were all right, and he looked almost sad, as if he were about to weep. It was over. The Bessarabian border lay ahead.

Mother did weep—but her tears were those of gratitude, more than anything else.

We rested that night, and the next, sensing intuitively that the Russians, having retaken the Ukraine, were resting, too.

PART THREE

eleven

We crossed the border into Bessarabia (now Moldavia) around the 7th of April—three months from the time we left Strukyvka. And things were finally beginning to look up: the weather was still chill, but the ground was drying out, so that less and less often did we have to get down to wrestle the spokes around through the mud. And so we made better time, covering as many as twenty kilometers in a day, without having to get up before sunrise and still being able to stop to find a place to sleep well before dark.

But the best thing by far was that it was no longer a case of going twenty hours a day and devil take the hindmost; the Russians were no longer in pursuit. Perhaps, after clearing the last remnants of the occupying forces from Soviet soil, they had no further interest in hunting down a few thousand un-armed civilians. Perhaps, after the carnage at the Dniester and the Bug, their thirst for blood was sated. Or maybe it was simply a matter of their being as exhausted as we were, and needing to give their supplies and communications a chance to catch up. Whatever the reason, all we knew was that they had suddenly let up.[1]

And now the cumulative impact of all that we had been through—of going for weeks on a few hours' sleep and almost no food—caught up with us in a rush, as if an invisible barrier had been let down. Mother became deathly ill, and the rest of us, even father, barely had the strength to look after her. For several days we just stopped where we

---

1. As it happened, it had nothing to do with the front-line troops at all. The decision had been made long before in the far-distant Kremlin. The main objective of the army groups under Zhukov, Koniev and Rokossovsky had been to cut off and destroy as much of the enemy's force as possible, before they could slip away into Poland. Once this was accomplished, all units were to re-group to the north for a multi-pronged assault on Poland. Actually, not quite all: a token force would remain behind to press on into Bessarabia and Romania, their primary purpose being to tie down as many enemy troops there as possible.

The thinking of the German High Command was, not surprisingly, quite similar (both Hitler and Stalin were interested in other sectors, and this corner of the war, at least, could for the moment be conducted rationally): Assuming that the Russians would be unwilling to expend the enormous time and energy necessary to breach the Carpathians, only a token force need be retained in Romania, to stiffen the resistance of the natives. Therefore, all personnel who had been able to extricate themselves from the debacle in the Ukraine were to report to Poland immediately for re-assignment, for the Polish corridor had to be defended at all costs. All Slavic evacuees in territories still under German control would continue to be shipped to the Fatherland as long as possible.

Thus has it always been one of the ironies of war: that an area so hotly contested on one day would be of only "token" interest the next.

were so that she could sleep and eventually her fever did break.

But it was the two girls, Lydia and Lida, who were in the worst condition of all. Their eyes were sunken back in their heads, and when they moved their arms, you could see how all the bones fitted together at the elbows. That was more or less true of all of us, but in little girls seven and eight, it was a particularly painful sight. True, we were beginning to find food now in abandoned farmhouses and homes—and had enough to eat, in fact, for the first time since we had been evacuated from our village half a year earlier. But I heard mother telling father one night that nothing would bring the girls back into health more quickly than fresh milk.

That night, just before I went to sleep under the wagon—when we couldn't find an abandoned house or barn, mother and the girls slept in the wagon, under the tarpaulin, while father, Alexei and I slept underneath—I did as I had grown accustomed to doing during the past months, whenever I thought of it, and there was time: I told myself the story of the Land of Milk and Honey. I knew the details by heart of course, but for variety's sake I would embellish them from time to time. And that night, in addition to the river that God had put there to ease pain and wash away fatigue, and the fruit whose goodness you could feel sliding down your throat and into your stomach (that part always made me feel good), I added a tin cup that was always full of milk. After all, it was called the Land of Milk and Honey, wasn't it?

The next morning, I woke up and looked through the spokes of the wheel—at a large brown eye looking back at me. Startled, I noted that the eye was in a brown-and-white face, that the face was that of a cow, and that the cow was obviously in need of being milked. I eased out from under my blanket very slowly, sidled up to the cow and put an arm around her neck, then joyously called to mother, who, since the only farms in the area were abandoned, and the cow's udders were dripping, proceeded to milk her. When she was through, she turned the cow loose, but the cow refused to leave and started following us when *we* left.

As it turned out, that cow had simply adopted us. She had come without collar or bell, and she would not leave, and so we just adopted her back and gave her the name Katya. She was not a very big cow at that. And except when we were on the road, we never had to tie her; we just called her, and she would come just as if she were a pet. She was very gentle, so that the milk she gave—as much as any full-sized cow, up to ten liters at a milking—was sweet.

April turned into May, and while we were supposed to be traveling in convoy—and there were still enough Germans around to tell us where we were supposed to go next and to make sure that we were headed there—father was never happy unless his was the lead wagon. And so it was here, except that we were about a *week* in the lead. We were now passing through a series of what had once been German colonies before the occupants had been advised by their own soldiers that if they wanted to stay alive, they had better return at once to the Fatherland. Consequently, the scavenging had never been so good, another reason why father preferred to be a little ahead of the rest.

In the large, abandoned farmhouses, it became like a game to see who could find what for whom—a dress for Lida, leather boots for Alexei, a long coat for father, a pocketknife for me. By the time we reached the Siretul River in Romania, we were better fed, clothed and other-wise equipped than we had ever been in our lives.

And we were happy. The weather was getting warmer all the time, our wagon was well-stocked and in good shape, and our horses looked better than they ever had. And now that we had Katya with us, the girls were beginning to fill out. One morning, I even heard father singing (though that may have been due to the wine barrel in the cellar of the last house we visited). The scenery (we had time to notice the scenery now) was breathtaking. Ahead of us loomed the snow-capped Carpathians, and for a family that had spent its life on the steppes, they were quite a sight. In addition, the flowers were beginning to come out, and the grass was greening, and the gently rolling hills seemed to add a lilt to the horses' pace. It wasn't long before we were *all* singing.

Like gypsies, I mused, a gypsy family with no cares, answering the call of the open road. I tried to remember what Babunia had said about gypsies, but the moment she came into my mind, everything else left. How she would have loved to have been here with us! It was warm enough for her now, and there was plenty of food, and best of all, she would have seen the family as it was now—happy and well, but above all, together, as it had never been before—a *family.*

The nightmare we had been through had done that, although there was something more to it than that, something really important, but I couldn't get what it was. Recalling the nightmare, I had to admit that mother and father had been right: Babunia would not have survived. It occurred to me then that it was bothering me less and less to admit that father was right about things, and I imagined that that would have especially pleased Babunia.

Again I longed for her to be there, and the thought came to me that in a sense she was—and had been all along.

The convoy caught up to us as we turned north along the

Siretul. One of the wagons was driven by a large, flabby man named Grigory, whose wife Sonya had recently given birth to twins, and who was badly in need of some of Katya's milk, which we gladly gave him. He was also in need of someone to help him handle his horses, as he had no sensitivity to animals, and they would not respond to him.

Since I did seem to have a way with animals, father told me to travel in Grigory's wagon and drive his horses for him, which I did, though I got a bad feeling about Grigory and his wife, sensing that they resented us and everything about us, even as they were all smiles and went on and on about how grateful they were for the milk, and what a wonderful driver I was for a boy so young. I tried to tell father why I didn't want to be with them, but he would hear none of it: he had decided to help them for the twins' sake, and that was that. I resigned myself to the fact that I would be riding with them the rest of the trip, which, fortunately, was not that long. We had crossed over to the west bank of the Siretul a few days earlier and continued north till we reached its tributary, the river Sian, around the middle of May. This, it turned out, was our destination: the final assembly point. Across the Sian was the town of Adjud, the railhead of the last remaining line still open to Poland and Germany. There, as transportation became available, we would be shipped out. In the meantime, we were to take our place with the other convoys, waiting on the broad, high plain on the south side of the Sian.

But first the Germans meticulously recorded all posessions that we would not be taking with us—our wagons, horses, livestock, etc. These we would be responsible for until the actual day of departure, at which time they were to be turned over to the Germans. For each item we would be given a receipt, redeemable upon "cessation of hostilities"—provided Germany won, of course, though none of us was so impolite as to point that out.

And so, left pretty much alone by the Germans, we set up camp. And that's really what it was, a little city of wagons and tent-like tarpaulin shelters, or even blankets stretched over a bit of line. And for the next few days we did the things that one does in camp—mending clothes, washing laundry down by the river, but mainly just resting. For while the children and younger adults had recuperated fairly quickly from the nightmare, for those who were older, it would be a long time before their systems regained their resiliency—and many never would.

Finally, the word was passed: the transportation had arrived, and we would be embarking tomorrow. All possessions were to be turned in first thing in the morning. That meant our beloved Katya—and the thought of turning her over to the Germans was more than we could bear. And not only us, for throughout the entire camp, she had made friends who loved her as we did. Well, not quite the entire camp—two days before, in her wandering, she had paused to see what was going on at Grigory and Sonya's wagon. What was going on was that Sonya was making bread, and her dough had just begun to rise in a big earthen pot that she had set in the sun behind their wagon. Katya had sniffed the dough and eaten it, every bit of it, with great relish, according to Grigory, who was obviously incensed and yet was trying to act as if he found it amusing, since his twins were among those children in the camp who were receiving Katya's milk twice a day.

I pleaded with father not to give Katya to the Germans who would slaughter her for meat as quickly as possible.

"What can I do," he snapped back, "when the Germans have 'one cow' listed after the name Basansky?"

"Well, you'll think of something; you always do."

He scowled at this unusual acknowledgment and said nothing, but I sensed he was pleased. In his own way, as much as he was able, father loved Katya, too, and so that afternoon, he put a lead on her and took her away. When he came back several hours later, he had a sack with two bottles of vodka in it, a pocket full of money, and a year-old heifer in tow. I asked him none of the details, but I was very happy. And so was everyone else.

Except Grigory. When he came by and wanted to know where his milk was, for Alexei and I had made no deliveries that afternoon, he saw the heifer and put two and two together. Furious, he had told father that he had no right to do what he did. Father just shook his head in disgust and walked away.

That evening in camp, there was a feeling of sadness, of termination. We had been through so much, and the last days had given us back hope and life. No one knew what tomorrow held in store—what awaited us in Germany, whether we would be separated, whether we would ever get there at all. We just sensed that it would never be the same again.

Whenever Ukrainians feel that way, their remedy is celebration, and celebration means food. That afternoon everyone had more or less spontaneously decided to cook whatever supplies they had left (there was no point in turning it in to the Germans). For several hours stew-pots had been simmering all over the camp, and now the smell of baking bread mingled with the rich aroma of goulash.

"Hey! Dreamer!" my father shouted at me, "why haven't these horses been watered?"

I hurried to take *Vorona*, the black mare, down to the river. By the time I got back, and was leading *Risha*, the red mare, the sun had already set, but the western sky was still light—shades of red-purple surrounded by a clear wash of blue that was fast darkening into blue-black and night. All those cooking fires now stood out brightly in the gathering dusk, and were surrounded by silhouettes squatting or sitting on the ground.

The scene reminded me of the bands of gypsies that used to stop at the outskirts of our village in the summer. Mother had forbidden us to go near them—everyone knew that gypsies stole little children—but Alexei and I had to find out more about them and would watch them from hiding. During the day they would slip into town, begging food, beguiling the women with their flashing smiles, the older children with their tales, and the old men with their clever tongues, and generally casting a spell over the whole village, till people gave them far more than they intended to, and hardly seemed to mind if they were suddenly missing a day's eggs or their cow had been milked dry.

One afternoon I'd caught a glimpse of an old gypsy woman ducking around the corner of a neighbor's house, and following at what I thought was a safe distance, all at once I practically ran into her, for she had been waiting for me. She just stared at me, and her eyes, deep and black, made me feel all hollow inside, and alone and very much afraid. Looking into those eyes, I would have given her anything of mine she asked for.

I had broken free from her gaze and run home, and did not sneak back with Alexei to watch their campfire that night. Thinking of that now, something made me recall a scene that I had been trying not to remember. The night that I had nearly frozen to death after we'd crossed the Ingulets, it had rained. And the rain had turned to sleet and then to snow, so that in the morning there was a sheet of snow-covered ice over everything. We all were under the tarpaulin in the wagon, in an old barn, the roof of which was lifting and banging in the wind, all of which actually helped father to keep awake and keep him from freezing solid.

In the morning, it was overcast, and we had difficulty climbing the road behind the barn, because of the ice and snow. As we reached the top of the rise, we came upon a band of gypsies. They were lying in a circle, and every one was frozen in the position in which they had fallen asleep—except one with an arm upraised, who must have realized what was happening to them too late to really get moving.

As my horror wore off, I had wondered at the time why that should happen to them and not to us, and now I remembered what it was that Babunia had said about the gypsies: that their power came from the Evil One himself, and that I was not to have anything to do with them. It had made me sad at the time, for Alexei and I had just been to watch their campfire, and their dancing was unlike any I had ever seen. The black and crimson skirts of their women would flash and rise in the firelight as they spun faster and faster, and the racing music of their violins and tambourines would soar ever higher till it seemed it would pull you right into it.

And then, all at once the dance would be over, and the dancers would be laughing and gasping for breath. And for grown-ups who dared to enter their wagons, there would be palm-reading and Tarot cards and perhaps a crystal ball. And that night the village would have strange dreams. In the morning, the gypsies would be gone without a trace, and you would almost wonder if you had imagined them—until you found no egg under your hen. Or no hen. . . .

I turned and walked Risha down the bank to the river's edge. Above, on the plain, I caught the strains of a guitar and then an accordion. And singing, which meant that the celebration now included vodka, wine and cognac from Romanian cellars. And that meant there would soon be dancing.

"Come on, Risha, drink," I urged her, anxious to get back. But she would not be hurried. I had brought her last, because I had taught her to jump, and was looking forward to riding her back. Finally, she finished, and I leapt astride her and charged up the slope and onto the plain.

The music had spread like wildfire through the camp, and now everyone was singing and dancing *Hopak,* and I knew my father would be kicking better than all the rest. The music seemed to be in Risha, too, as she lengthened her gait, till soon we were flying through the night, her hooves drumming on the ground and me hunched forward, right behind her neck, in the best tradition of the Zaporozhye Cossacks. I gave a long war cry, which encouraged her even more, and as we approached the camp, I began looking for jumps—first the tongue of a wagon—then a barrel—and then, right over Grigory's cooking fire.

I cleared it easily, but Sonya started crying and carrying on, so I wheeled Risha back and got down to apologize. As I walked up to Grigory, he grabbed me and started smacking me around, really laying into me.

I didn't realize it, but my father, who had seen it all, now came running over, grabbed Grigory's shoulder, spun him around, and hit him so hard he took several steps backward and sat down. But he was up quickly, for Grigory was large enough to be a bully and didn't realize that my father had enough meanness in him to handle a man three times his size. My father had long ago learned how to punish a man as much as possible with each blow, and soon Grigory went reeling back through his own cooking fire, taking pots, yoke and kettle with him.

Such was the commotion that the Germans had no choice but to step in, taking Grigory and father aside and starting to question them. Father's German was not intelligible, but Grigory's was, and now he got even, not only for the beating, but for all the grievances he had been nursing for weeks. He told the Germans that father had cheated them, trading the cow that he had reported, for a heifer and money.

To the Germans, this was a grave offense—a shooting offense—and the officer in command, drew his pistol. I knew there was no point in trying my old trick of interposing myself, that in fact, there was nothing I could do but stand there with the others and watch. But someone else did do something: a man in our convoy whom we didn't even know but who spoke fluent German stepped up to the officer and told him that Grigory did not know the whole truth. The truth, according to this man, was that the cow had broken its leg and had had to be put down, and my father, afraid not to turn one in, had then gone and purchased the heifer. Grigory had said what he did just to get even for my father's coming to my aid.

So calm and straightforward was this presentation that the officer chose to believe him over Grigory, who was now screaming that my father and the stranger were in collusion. The officer ordered them both to go to their wagons without another word, warning them not to fight again.

When they were out of earshot of the officer, the stranger said to father, "Sorry to have stretched the truth that way, but I just couldn't let him get away with having you shot." My father shook his hand, and then put his arm around my shoulder, and we walked back to our wagon. Tears sprang to my eyes, and I looked away so that he wouldn't see them.

In the camp, the fires had burned low, and now someone started to sing, one of the saddest songs we knew, and one voice after another joined in until the whole plain seemed to echo the refrain. And now I no longer had to hide my tears, for there were tears in every eye we passed.

twelve

In the morning, it was overcast, and on a rail-siding outside of Adjud, our transportation awaited us: a string of cattle-cars too long to count. The shock of the sight hit all of us like a physical blow, and as if to emphasize it, the Germans were now herding us along, cramming as many as possible into each car, then closing the door and bolting it shut from the outside, and moving us on to the next.

"Alexei, Vasili!" father commanded hurriedly, "each of you take one of the girls by the hand and stick as close to us as you can. Whatever happens, make sure that we get in the same car!" I grabbed Lida, and Alexei, Lydia, and we pressed up behind mother and father. As soon as they climbed up, we handed the girls up to them, and got up ourselves. And almost immediately the door slammed shut behind us.

It took awhile for our eyes to get accustomed to the darkness, for the only light was from the spaces between the boards. The car had a large bucket in the corner for sanitary purposes, some straw on the floor, and that was all. Into the car were crammed twice as many people as there were places to sleep, and by the time we had gotten aboard, all the space was taken. But this turned out to be extremely providential, for in that drafty car, the only place where we were even partially protected was with our backs up against the forward end of the car—something which became apparent only after we had gotten underway.

All told, we spent three weeks in that car—in a nightmare of a different sort than the one we had gone through before. At least, getting out of the Ukraine, we had had freedom of movement. Here, we were at the mercy of whoever threw open that door. And the only time it was opened was when we were shunted on to a siding, where we waited sometimes for hours for an ammunition train to roar past, bound for the front. At such times, the Germans would let us go out into the fields, to forage for whatever we could find. But they did not let us go on the other side of the train, and stood with submachine guns watching us.

We brought back straw, and occasionally someone would be lucky enough to find an unharvested potato or some corn, but for the most part, it was another starving time. I wished, of course, that we were back on the plain above the Sian, but, I think for the first time in my life, I was also grateful—that we had had that time, that chance for body and mind to recuperate.

Alexei and I would press our faces against the cracks to get a glimpse of where we were going, but the rolling countryside seemed to repeat itself, like a beautiful but forbidden fantasy, of ancient mountains, green meadows, and sparkling brooks, unfolding on the other side of the slatted boards of the cattle-car. Inside the car, the days and nights ran together in a blur, till the only indication of time

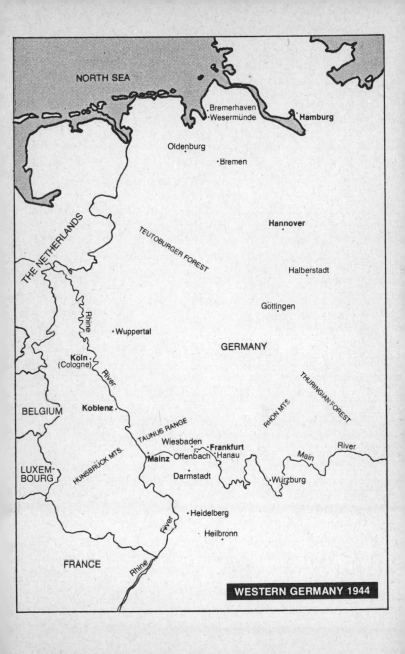

WESTERN GERMANY 1944

passing was people's colds getting worse and turning into pneumonia, people's nerves getting worse and tempers flaring up, and the stench from the overflowing sanitary bucket getting so bad (there was no door or window to empty it through) that we finally broke a hole in the floor of the car. And then, when I thought I was about to just scream and beat my head against the wall (as one or two others already had), the journey was over—at least for the moment.

We had reached Przemysl in Poland, where other cattle trains were arriving, and where the final disbursement of Slav labor was to be made. The first thing they did was to have us take off all our clothes and walk down a long corridor. At the end, clouds of vapor billowed out of a room. Suddenly the word *gas* was whispered back along the line. But it turned out to be showers, after which they kept us waiting all day, naked and shivering in the cold corridors, from which many caught pneumonia, and in a few days were dead. Finally, we were doused with disinfectant powder, given back our clothes and taken before a *kommisia*—a committee, to be assigned.

Again we were given the opportunity to volunteer to fight the Russians, and other able-bodied men and older boys were simply shipped to the front, to dig and do other heavy labor as required. But most of the men that remained were there because they were the heads of families with three or more children twelve and under (for which reason, Alexei and I each had a year lopped off our ages, whenever father reported). Some of these families were separated, some were allowed to remain together, and any Jews who had somehow slipped through previous nets were sent— somewhere else.

Babunia would have said that God had His hand over us, for once again, the Basansky family was able to stay together, and three days later we got back in another cattle-car, arriving at our final destination on July 4, 1944: the labor camp at Mainz. As we walked through the main gates, the guards on the lookout towers looked down on us, and every one was wearing the black uniform of the SS.

Now, for the first time, we were separated: men to the left, women to the right, and children twelve and under, straight ahead. At least Alexei and I would be able to look after the girls, I thought. Our camp was specifically for *Auslanders*—foreigners, meaning Poles, White Russians and Ukrainians. Located on the peninsula of the Main and Rhine Rivers, the camp took up the space of about a city block, and next to it was another camp of French and English prisoners-of-war, whose rations we were to envy, and whom we could occasionally see opening parcels from home brought by the Red Cross.

Directly across the Main from us, literally under a mountain, was a munitions works that was rumored to be the largest in Germany, and on our other side was the M.A.N. factory which made parts for airplane fuselages and also for pre-assembled bridge sections. (When a bridge was bombed out, all the Germans had to do was replace the ruined sections; they could often have it back in operation in a matter of hours.) They needed welders for this work and started training father the day we arrived. Alexei and I were assigned to work on a nearby farm, and mother was put to work in the kitchen. The girls joined the younger children in cleaning up the camps.

Life in the camp was an endless procession of gray days with not enough food and nights tormented by bedbugs that seemed to live inside the wood of the boards we slept on and would leave us covered with sores by morning. There was no way we could combat them; the only thing that seemed to work was fire, but after experimenting with smuggled matches and nearly setting the barracks on fire, we soon gave up.

Once again, it became a question of how badly did we

want to live, for people in our camp were starving to death. And again our instinct for survival and all our experience was tried to the limit. In the factory, father would pocket pieces of plastic and a small saw. With these, he would fashion combs and trade them to the women of the camp for bread.

In the kitchen, when they soaked the potatoes in water, starch would settle to the bottom of the vats, and mother would scrape this off and with it mix the dregs of the ersatz coffee made from ground barley. On the farm, Alexei and I were occasionally able to pilfer tobacco, which we would smuggle into the camp, and which we would then trade for food. And so we survived.

But our health deteriorated, along with everyone else's. Mother developed rheumatoid arthritis; I became infested with worms. I could feel them moving inside of me—in my intestines, my stomach and eventually even into my throat, until I thought I would choke. There was nothing I could do to get rid of them, nor was the camp about to provide any medication—I was hardly the only person suffering from them. So, I learned to live with them.

About the only bright thing in our existence, literally, were the planes. Silver bombers came over in such numbers that they stretched from horizon to horizon, as if a glittering, see-through curtain had been drawn across the sky. At first, German fighters, grey-green with black crosses on the wings, would soar up from Wiesbaden to meet them, but these in turn were met by other silver planes—fighters with white stars in a circle on the wings—which seemed from the ground to be a little faster. In the few minutes before the high bombers came overhead, on their way to Frankfurt, and other industrial centers north and east of us, these planes would arc and loop and dive, filling the sky with their trails. On each succeeding encounter there were fewer interceptors to go aloft, until by January, when Mainz itself became the bombers' primary objective, there were so few that they seldom went up at all.

As the first planes came over, instead of dropping bombs, they dropped little strips of a metallic substance (which I learned years later was aluminum foil, dropped to confuse the enemy's anti-aircraft radar). And then the bombs would fall. Despite the camouflage paint and netting over the M.A.N. factory, the silver bombers seemed to know exactly where it was, and the precision of their bombing was breathtaking. Regular bombs didn't seem to do that much damage, but the incendiaries that they dropped by parachute at night would burn their way right through the steel roof and girders, and by the end of February, 1945, the factory was totally destroyed.

Another indication of their accuracy was that, in all that time, only two bombs fell inside of our camp: the first happened to fall squarely on that part of the barracks which was occupied by Slavic informers (separated from the rest of us for their own protection), and the second fell right at the open mouth of our shelter—and did not go off. Coincidence? Babunia would not have said so. And looking at that huge bomb buried right up to its fins, I was beginning to know in my heart that she was right. Had it exploded, it would have killed most of us, for our shelter was nothing more than two giant concrete drainage culverts, open at both ends and half-buried in a trench. (For themselves, the Germans had a bunker several feet thick, with a conical roof on it designed to shed bombs like rain.)

Even though it was obvious that the M.A.N. factory was pinpointed, to maintain the semblance of camouflage, we were under strict orders to stay in the culverts until the all-clear was sounded, so that no movement would be visible from the air. And just to make sure that that order was complied with, the camp commandant himself would be up in one of the guard towers with a telescopic rifle, ready for "target practice."

This man was typical of what we had come to expect from the SS. He had a farm not far away, on which he raised hogs, among other things. These he would feed with the peelings of the potatoes that were the staple of our diet, and an open wagon would come and take them out by the barrelful. Such was the hunger in the camp that the sight of all those peelings going by was enough to cause a man to ignore everything and just reach out for a handful. What he was ignoring was five to ten lashes with a lead-filled rubber hose and three days in solitary confinement without food or water. Women offenders received additional punishment: their heads were shaven.

But it was almost as if the commandant invited such infractions, for there was also, down the center of the open area in the middle of the camp, a mound of potatoes buried under the earth and packed with straw to protect them in winter. These potatoes were likewise *verboten,* but the children in the camp were allowed to play on the mound, and we all knew what was under there. One day, when I thought no one was watching, I quickly plunged my arm down into soil I had loosened, felt around, and came up with a rotten potato. My delight vanished as I looked up to see two glistening black boots standing right next to me—the commandant was smiling; he would administer this punishment himself. And so I was taken to his office, where he proceeded to beat me with an iron rod.

Most punishment, however, was given out by the one man in camp whose sadism rivaled the commandant's, a man who was one of us, but who, for special treatment and for a double portion of food, was in charge of administering all punishment and delighted in every stroke of the hose, delivered usually to victims who were first made to take a cold shower and lie down on the cement shower floor. On the other hand, almost as if to deliberately foil any attempt at generalization, the man who was second in command of the camp—who was also an SS officer and who used to walk around with a swagger stick and a fierce looking German shepherd—was a decent and humane individual. When he was certain that he could not be observed by any of the guards or informers (or the informers' informers, for he knew who they were, too), he would do certain kindnesses, like slipping the children cookies. That may not seem like much—until you consider what would happen to him, if he got caught.[1]

As the months went by, the biggest change took place not in the camp, but in what was going on overhead, for the sky above told the story. When we had come in July of '44, the bombers passed over so high that they were little more than silver specks, and they came maybe once every two or three days. Each time, the swarm of interceptors that rose to meet them was slightly diminished, and so were the number of anti-aircraft batteries. In those early days, the sky would be thick with black puffs of smoke, and from time to time we would see a bomber start streaking smoke and fall out of formation, its crew bailing out and sometimes machine-gunned from the ground as they hung in their harnesses. But as the months went by, the flak bursts became fewer and fewer, until there were almost none at all.

Conversely, the raids became more frequent and greater

---

1. After the war, when this man and the Russian informer were both brought to trial for war cimes, former inmates of the camp came forward to give their testimony. The vice-commandant was acquitted; the Russian received life imprisonment.

in size, until they were coming day and night, and because of the absence of flak, they were coming in lower than ever. This was particularly true when they started coming for Mainz itself, for the M.A.N. factory and the munitions works, and also for the V-2 rocket sites northeast of us. We used to marvel at the sight of those V-2's, in the fall of '44, as they rose majestically straight up, until almost leisurely they leaned over and streaked away to the west.

Now the planes were coming so low that we had no trouble reading the big white star in the circle with the two flaps extended. Those of us who dared to look out of the culvert could see their bomb-bay doors opening, and a string of bombs falling out, wobbling at first, like fledgling birds learning how to fly, then plummeting straight and true to their targets. I didn't know who was in those silver bombers, or what country had sent them; all I knew was that I had a tremendous yearning to be with them. I longed to be lifted right up out of the camp and installed in one of them, even knowing the risk involved.

It wasn't long before the M.A.N. factory was finished, and the V-2 rockets flew no more. But the munitions works across the river were another matter. No matter what they tried, day or night, the bombers could not seem to penetrate the exterior of that mountain. One Sunday, we children were permitted to go to the river's edge to play, and I was fascinated to have a closer look at the hive of activity across the way. Our brief glimpse into what lay beyond the huge, sliding-steel doors disclosed a vast, lighted corridor through which an endless stream of trucks arrived to pick up heavy ammunition—shells, bombs, torpedoes—and departed at all hours of the day and night, for the banks of work lights were only extinguished when the sirens began to wail.

Lower and lower, the bombers came, till it almost seemed

as if they were trying to fling their bombs straight at the massive steel doors. And then one night during a raid, the earth was shaken by a tremendous explosion. Ignoring the order about staying in the culverts, a number of us climbed out to watch, for the explosion had become two and then three and four.

Across the river, a mountain was being torn asunder. Huge hunks of it were lifted into the air, revealing a white-hot inferno within, while at the same time, the doors were gone, and great spouts of flame belched out. And then, in one last, cataclysmic eruption, the entire top of the mountain lifted off, and the molten essence of its interior exploded in the heavens turning night into day.

And it was over

thirteen

Two weeks later, they threw open the gates of the camp and ordered us out. *"Raus, raus! Schnell!"* On the double, we were hustled out of the camp and down the road. The Basansky family was re-united again, even if it was at a half-trot. What did it mean? Someone said that they had heard a guard say that we were going to Heidelberg. But someone else who knew the country, or who had seen a map, said that no, Heidelberg was south, and we seemed to be going east, paralleling the Main, not the Rhine, which meant we were going to Frankfurt.

As usual, no one really knew *where* we were going, and the rumor mills were grinding overtime: they were moving us to avoid the embarrassment of our being liberated (for by this time, March 16, 1945, no one had any illusions about the imminence of the Allied victory—even a fool could read the signs in the sky). They were taking us far enough out of the city to kill us without leaving any evidence. They were about to be overrun by the Americans and didn't know what to do with us (which was probably the closest to the truth). I fervently hoped it *was* the Americans; as bad as the camp was, to be liberated by the Russians meant that our execution was assured; at least in the camp we were still alive. And as I thought about that, it came to me that the *only* way we could have survived as long as we had, was for everything to have happened to us exactly as it had. If we had not been betrayed at the cave, if we had not been in this labor camp, the Russians would surely have killed us as collaborators. And despite everything, we *were* still alive. I thought of Babunia then. . . .

For the next two days we were moved at a quick march, until we reached the outskirts of Hanau, just beyond Frankfurt and Offenbach. There, we were taken into the woods and told to sit down. And now the grist was really ground out: this was it. Any minute now, and a truck with a heavy machine-gun in it would back in here and let us have it. And no sooner had that word spread, then, sure enough, along came a truck with an SS officer riding in it. But the officer turned out to be the vice-commandant, and the truck contained a meal of hot soup and bread that he had had the camp prepare for us, far better fare than they usually served us, and we sat down hungrily to consume it. When we finished and looked around, the truck, the vice-commandant and our guards had vanished. We were alone.

We couldn't believe it at first and thought it was some Nazi trick; and it was a long time before any of us got up and started to walk around. "Don't do it," someone said, "they're just waiting for an excuse to shoot us all for 'trying to escape.' You're going to get us all killed."

But we could hear shooting in the distance—it seemed to be coming from the other side of the Main—and father, Alexei and I sensed that they had really just dumped us, and the coast was clear. So we and two other families started edging away from the woods and down a road that passed by a cemetery. This suddenly struck us as an ideal place to hide—and so it proved to be. From behind the gravestones, we could occasionally see Germans walking by with sub-machine guns—and running, as the tempo of small-arms fire increased.

Then after two days, all at once it became quiet, and people began hanging white bedsheets of surrender out their windows everywhere we looked. A jeep drove by that we could see was not Russian, and then an American G.I. walked up behind us with a big grin on his face and a Hershey bar in his hand. It turned out he was Polish and could understand us, and when he heard that we hadn't eaten in two days, except for what we were able to beg, he said for us to wait right there, and that he would soon be back. In the meantime, I took my first bite of chocolate—I couldn't believe what my mouth was telling me! Could anything taste so sweet?

The American returned with, of all things, a sheep that he had shot, and we had a regular feast! As we finished all that we could eat, he asked us what we were going to do, and we said we didn't know. Then he told us that he had heard that they were establishing a DP camp on the way to Offen-bach, and maybe they could help us there. A DP camp, I learned, was a camp for Displaced Persons, a term we were to become well familiar with during the next four years.

At the DP camp, they didn't have room for us, so they bivouacked us across the street, in a three-story house that we shared with several other families. In back of the camp was a rail-yard, in which a number of cars had been bombed and derailed. These were soon picked over by the DP's, who discovered several tank cars of wood alcohol, and two box cars full of small arms and ammunition—Lugers, grenades, dynamite, even submachine-guns.

The combination proved lethal. Whereas a few days before, we had had to beg food from the German civilians while on the march or hiding out in Hanau, often to be rebuffed or have doors slammed in our faces (I had dogs sicked on me outside of Frankfurt and was even shot at by some still-avid Nazis), now we took what we needed at gunpoint. We would go by a farm, and if we saw a pig that we wanted, we'd just take it. And if the farmer started hollering at us, we'd throw a stick of dynamite at him. For some of the more bitter DP's, this became a time of getting even and settling scores, a time of lawlessness that got pretty ugly, until there was little difference between some of the present doers-unto, and the meanest of those who had been doing unto us.

But for Alexei and me, it was more like the old war games we used to play before the real war came to our village. Only now, instead of sticks for guns and rocks for grenades, we had the real thing. And so, tearing around and just shooting for fun of it, we learned how to handle weapons and dynamite.

Actually, the opposite was the truth, as far as the dynamite was concerned: we learned how *not* to handle it. The dynamite had three basic ingredients: the dynamite itself, which would not go off alone, and was shaped like a brick with a hole in the middle for a cap; the metallic percussion cap, which blew up the brick; and the fuse, which set off the percussion cap. We treated the bricks like they were giant firecrackers, and the percussion caps we would stick fuses in and light them, and then see how long we dared hold them before letting go, and if we could hit the ground before they exploded. One boy had one go off and send its metal into his face, and I once got a piece of metal in my chest, but still we didn't learn.

Another near-tragedy involving dynamite was when we decided to blast for fish in the Main. Alexei, I, and a friend of ours named Sergei took the dynamite, caps and fuses down to the river in a baby carriage so as not to attract attention, and we had a rubber raft, in which Sergei and I launched forth with our explosives, commando-style. The raft was so small that we agreed that each would sit on his own side and stay there, no matter what, to keep from tipping over.

We lit the fuses of *two* bricks of dynamite, eased them into the water so as not to startle the fish, and then paddled away and waited. The fuse was designed to burn under water, and ten seconds after we had sent it down, there was a muffled *ka-room* and a large part of the river mushroomed up behind us. So did a great many dead fish, which we gleefully proceeded to scoop up until our raft was more than half-full. And then I spotted it, trailing inquisitively along behind us—the biggest carp that Sergei or I had ever seen!

Well, there was no question about it: we had to get that fish! He was so big that he must have thrown a lot of hooks in his life, but I was sure he'd never encountered dynamite before. Yet we had to move very slowly; the slightest start could spook him. Carefully I drew my pocketknife, and with the eye of a seasoned sub-chaser, cut a fuse that would last about three seconds—just long enough for him to nose up to it, to see what it was.

I gave Sergei the thumbs-up signal, and we almost convulsed with silent laughter. And then I lit the fuse and let the brick go into the water. Almost instantly there was a tremendous *ka-bam* which nearly set our raft up on end. It did upset the carp, who turned belly up, and was even bigger on the surface than he had appeared beneath.

Whooping with joy, Sergei was so excited to see our kill that he came over to my side of the raft, and the next thing we knew, we were both in the water, the raft was upside down and out of reach, and all the dynamited fish were floating away.

Our raft was drifting away in the swift current of the river, but that didn't bother Sergei, who was still laughing and who was headed for shore, assuming that I was right behind him. I wasn't. I had on heavy boots, laced up, and a woolen jacket that soaked up water like a sponge and started pulled me under.

On the shore, Alexei was watching: "Now look what you've done, Durak!" he called out, "Our raft, and all those fish. . . ." and then he realized that I was in trouble. Shucking off his clothes, he dived in and got to me before I went under again. Pulling me safely ashore, he got dressed and ran downriver and across a bridge to where the raft had fetched up on the other side. Then, while I sheepishly built a fire to dry my clothes, he gathered up as many fish as he could find, including the great carp.

That evening, when we got back with our baby carriage full of fish, father was delighted with our catch, and promptly traded most of them (though not the carp) for more wood alcohol, for Russians and Ukrainians love fish, and it had been a long time since anyone had seen any. Wood alcohol is deadly of course, and we knew that, but Ukrainians are almost deliberately hard-headed about that sort of thing. Knowing the danger, they proceeded to boil the alcohol, thinking that somehow that would take the poison out of it, and then, when people began to suffer ill effects, they also baked bread and strained the alcohol through that, hoping that *that* would purify it. It didn't, and people started going blind, including my father.

Did that stop him? He did lay off for a few days—nobody would give him any, and he couldn't see to get it himself—

and miraculously his vision returned, and the sickness set-tled instead in his legs, paralyzing him from the knees down. This slowed him down, but it didn't stop him. In the meantime, other people died from it, including our friend Sergei. That scared Alexei and me so badly that we never touched the stuff.

The best thing that happened to me during those three weeks in the DP camp was that I got delivered of my worms. Someone had told me that the way to get rid of them was to eat a lot of garlic and then not drink any water for two days. Then I was to expose them to water, and they would leave of their own accord. So I did. I chewed mouthfuls of green garlic cloves, and did that stir them up! I could feel them fairly churning around inside. When two days were up, I just went and sat on a toilet, and sure enough, they started crawling down out of me. I saved one to show to mother: it was thirty centimeters long.

But in general, our three weeks of freedom had turned into a binge. The Americans figured we had it coming, and pretty much turned their backs on our goings on. And now, soon after the Germans finally surrendered on May 8, 1945, the Russians appeared on the scene with a train that was going to take us all home, and backed it into the rail-yard in back of the camp.

Ukrainians are eternal optimists. Given the slightest straw of hope, they will grasp onto it and build a house out of it. With great fanfare, the Russians announced a general amnesty—all our offenses, whatever they were, were forgiv-en, our homes and relatives were awaiting us, and here at last was the train home to the Motherland! And many DP's climbed on the bandwagon, waving huge red banners with the hammer and sickle and singing the favorite songs of New Russia (not of Old Russia, for there were Commissars present, duly taking note of all proceedings). And having once convinced themselves that all had indeed been forgiv-en, and the Motherland awaited them with open arms, they did their best to convince others. The fervor caught hold, and soon the whole DP camp was drunk with homesickness and nostalgia, if not with alcohol (wood or otherwise)—remembering things, not as they had actually been, but as they had always wanted them to be. And some even went down to decorate the train with flowers and bunting, for in the morning, it would depart—full, with twin red flags flying from the front of the locomotive.

Drunk or sober, father was too much of a realist for all that. He knew that it was either go home or get out of that camp fast; there were too many Russian soldiers around already to suit him. And if he went home, he knew it was to the open arms of a firing squad, no matter how much they talked about amnesty. So, two days before the grand departure of the train, he slipped quietly out of the camp with the help of Lida and Lydia, and went to see a man he knew in Offenbach. Father could not walk, due to his paralysis, but he had enough control above the knees so that he could ride a bike, *if* someone helped him up on it. And then, if he were strapped on, he could go a fair distance. But if he ever fell, it was all over. Since it was fifteen kilometers, to Offenbach, the girls went with him.

He was going to see the man about a farm where we could work and at the same time hide from the Russians, for father had a strong intuition that it wouldn't be long before they would be looking for Ukrainians to take home—without songs and smiles.

That left just mother, Alexei and me in the house the night of the pre-departure celebration. When everyone was asleep or passed out, including the Russian soldier, who while the festivities were at their height, had been unobtrusively posted at the front door to make sure that no one left, we slipped down the stairs and made our getaway, wheeling our belongings in the baby carriage.

We were just coming out onto the street, when walking towards us we saw an American sentry. It was too late to duck back inside, too late to do anything but just keep on walking. Well, this is it, I thought, and I felt needles of fear lancing into me. He'll take us back, wake up the Russian, and turn us over to him, and that will be the end of it. But the American just passed us by, as if it were the most normal thing in the world for a mother and her sons to be taking a baby for some fresh air at 3:00 in the morning.

We reached the plain outside Offenbach, where father and the girls were waiting for us, and went together to a small farming village a few kilometers away. Going on down a wooded road for another couple of kilometers, eventually we reached a farm, the foreman of which spoke some Ukrainian. He was German-born, but his mother came from Galicia, and so we were able to communicate. Father gave him the name of the man who had sent him, and he nodded and advised us to go back to register and receive a work visa, after which the owner would be happy to hire us.

We spent nearly a year on that farm, during which time mother spent many months in the hospital in Offenbach, where she was extremely ill, not just with arthritis but with grave internal disorders, and the doctors had advised us that we should be prepared for her death. That was bad enough, but she was also in constant pain, with inflammation of the joints, for which there seemed to be no relief.

Father, too, was out of commission, having to go to the hospital several times a week for treatment of his paralysis, which left only Alexei and me able to do any real work on the farm. We did work, hard, and the owner was pleased with what we were doing and was happy enough to have the rest of the family there. That included mother, who was eventually well enough to come home, though far from able to work.

And so, life was tolerable, and then in the late fall, we had our first close call. As my father had anticipated, the Russian dragnet had begun.[1] Russian soldiers, with Allied approval, were systematically going through the work visa registrations of cities, towns, and villages, looking for DP's with Slavic names. But when they came to the village where our names were on record, incredibly our cards were missing! The only explanation that we could come up with, when we heard about it, was that the *burgermeister* had taken pity on us and removed our cards from the file before they could be found. But I knew Babunia would have another explanation, and I could just see her smiling and nodding her head.

The second close call came soon after that, when two Russian soldiers actually came to the farm. They were in a truck driven by a local German who could speak some Russian, and they were there to buy potatoes from the farmer. The foreman warned us in the nick of time to go to our rooms and stay there until he told us it was clear. We did go, looking through the curtains at them with our hearts racing, and there, for the first time, mother commanded us

---

1. In February of 1945, at Yalta, where the fate of post-war Eastern Europe was decided, Roosevelt agreed to Stalin's insistence that all citizens of the Soviet Union be repatriated—after all, why shouldn't people go home? But what America and her President could not know was what lay in store for *anyone* who had left the Soviet Union, whether by choice or exile, or by force, as evacuees or prisoners-of-war. Execution awaited many, and ten years in a Siberian labor camp was considered light. But we who had lived under the Communists, knew—and thus, while the word "forcibly" did not precede "repatriated" in the formal wording of the Agreement, that is what it amounted to. The Americans may not have believed the "distraught" DP's who tried to tell them, but the Russians understood perfectly, and so did we.

to pray with her, having us repeat the Lord's prayer after her. Before long, the Russians left.

The third close call came two days later, though this one we weren't aware of until much later, when the German driver told us what had happened. While the Russians had been at the farm, some of the other workers had told the driver that there was a Ukrainian family also working on the farm, and this he had happened to mention on the way back. The soldiers had to deliver their potatoes, but they were very interested and arranged for the German to take them back to the farm as soon as they could come back themselves, which would be in two days. When they returned, the German took them out the wooded road—but was unable to find the farm, though they drove up and down until there was no more light.

So fear was once again a part of the fabric of our lives, as omnipresent with us now, as it had been in the Ukraine, and it seemed like it had never really left. In addition, the owner of the farm had died, and his widow made it perfectly clear that she did not share her late husband's regard for us: she gave us food for only Alexei and myself, "since we were the only ones working."

And so, it was another survival situation, and by now Alexei and I were old hands at that. On the second floor of the building in which we lived was a large storage area for grain, dried peas and corn. But at the top of the stairs, in an apartment to the right, lived a bachelor who was the assistant foreman.

Getting into the storage area was no problem; all Alexei or I had to do was wait for the man upstairs to visit his girlfriend in the next town. But sometimes he would come home earlier than we expected him, and whoever was up there would wind up trapped in the storage area, with nothing to do but wait until he fell asleep—sound asleep.

Then it was a question of getting the grain downstairs, without getting caught red-handed. This we did by means of a bucket and a long rope, making use of the window at the opposite end of the building. Whoever was down below would wait for the bucket, and then all the second-story man had to do was open the sliding door to the stairs— without the creak that it almost always made.

We had one other means of supplementing our food supply; we were able to snare deer. We had never snared deer before, nor had anyone told us how, but we took the lessons that we had learned snaring rabbits back in the Ukraine, and followed the same procedure. Locating a deer trail, we would look for a jump, where whatever was on the other side would be naturally obscured. Telephone wire and a camouflaged loop did the rest. And we caught no less than three deer.

In short, the quality our life had gotten considerably less tolerable than when we arrived. Yet even so, when father came back from the hospital one day with reliable news of a first-class DP camp in Mainz, run by the Americans, with American food and above all, American medical facilities, and said that he wanted to go there, it very nearly caused a split in the family Basansky. Because, with his not being able to work, and with Alexei and I, in effect, providing for everyone, the leadership of the family had gravitated to us, even though we were only fourteen and fifteen. And to us, it seemed that as little as we had at the farm, at least it was something. And we had never really had anything before. Why throw it away for what was really just a hope?

But father kept coming back from the hospital and telling us more, and he won mother over, who was sick to death of the fear and of waking up every morning and wondering if that would be the day that the Russians came back. At least we would be under the Americans, instead of at the mercy of a woman who clearly despised us. That finally persuaded us, and so on April 20, 1946, we said goodbye and set off for the camp at Mainz-Kastel.

We thought we were saying goodbye to fear, too, but had hardly begun to make its acquaintance.

fourteen

The two best things about the camp at Mainz were the medical attention my father received, and the program they had for physically building up the DP children. My father began to be healed of his paralysis, to the point where he could walk, after a fashion, enough to hold a job, though he still had no muscle control below the ankles. And Lida, Lydia, Alexei and I all received quantities of dried milk and dried eggs, and were given a tablespoon of cod liver oil three times a day. (It tasted so awful, you knew it had to be good for you.)

The worst thing was that the Russian presence was infinitely more menacing here than it had ever been at the farm. For here, all the vague, unknown, gnawing fears that we had experienced before, now became stark, identifiable realities. The day we got to the camp, father met Mikhail, who had been at the first DP camp with us.

"What are you doing here?" Father asked, "I thought

you'd be home by now, or more likely serving time in Siberia. Didn't you go on that train, the one with all the flags?"

"I went on it."

"Well?"

Mikhail obviously did not want to go on, but father persisted, and finally he got it out. "A lot of people on the train were hung over, when it pulled out. But the best way to cope with that is more vodka, and there was plenty of that on board. Before too long, everybody was singing again and laughing and crying to be going home." He paused and looked at the ground, sighting along the instep of his shoe. Father said nothing, and Mikhail finally looked up. "We weren't ten minutes inside the Russian Zone, when they stopped the train and ordered us out. No smiles now. Submachine-guns. *Nothing had changed!*" and he shook his head, whether in disbelief or at his own credulity, father couldn't say.

"They had been expecting us. The heavy machine guns were set up and loaded. *The pit was already dug!*" and he fought to keep control of himself. "They herded us all like cattle up in front of it, and opened fire."

Father waited.

"I'm here," he managed, "because even though I was only wounded, I fell back in the pit, and someone else fell on top of me, but from where I lay, I could see one of the gunners: he was smoking a cigarette. I kept still until it was safe to crawl out," he concluded flatly. "As far as I know, I was the only one."

When father told us about it later, none of us could believe it at first; it took time for the enormity of it to sink in. But he had other things to tell us as well, that helped. Apparently the Russians had been driving right into this camp with trucks, ostensibly to see if any Soviet citizens would like free transportation home, guaranteeing amnesty, to all who accepted, and reminding those with families or plots of land that it would soon be time to get this year's crops in.

But in reality, since everyone was on to them by this time, what they were doing was simply coming in with soldiers and manhandling people into the trucks at gunpoint and taking them. And outside the camp, they were cruising the American Zone in trucks and just scooping up any Slavs they happened to come across. People all over were disappearing in these trucks into the Russian Zone, never to be seen or heard from again. And it was all perfectly "legal," under the terms of the Yalta Agreement.

But two things happened, both a couple of months before we got there, that promised to bring a ray of hope. First, a DP took his family over to the American consulate, and right on the front steps took out a straight razor and slit the throats of his children, his wife, and himself, leaving a note that said, "I choose to die on freedom's doorstep than be sent back to be tortured to death in Russia."

This apparently shocked quite a few people, and when the identical thing happened a week later, an investigation was begun. About the same time, the Russians came back into the DP camp with their trucks one time too many. When they started heaving men into their trucks, the men refused to go. The Russians tried to brazen it through, but there were too many now who had had enough and were ready to die right there, if need be. In fact, there were so many that they beat up the Russians, threw them in their own vehicles, and pushed them into the Rhine.

So now the Americans finally began to realize that perhaps all was *not* as it appeared and that they had better take a closer look at things. That was where matters stood, when we arrived at Mainz at the end of April, 1946. From here, the farm we had been on didn't look so bad.

I missed the next episode; I was in town, buying some

bread, when it happened. When I got back, there was a ring of American half-tracks and jeeps around the camp. What had just taken place, I learned, was that there had been a line-up of the entire camp, and the Russians who had been beaten up and thrown in the Rhine had gone down the lines, accompanied by American officers, and picked out the individuals who had been involved. It should be added that when word spread through the camp that this identification was going to take place, several people hanged themselves, rather than face the possibility that they might be taken by the Russians.

The Russians did want to take with them all those whom they had identified, but the Americans said no, that since it had happened on territory for which they were responsible, they would do the trying of them. The Russians grew furious at that and demanded that the Americans turn them over immediately. The Americans did not back down but now took a special interest in seeing that the trial was conducted fairly and in what it would reveal.

The proceedings lasted six months, all told. What came out was that a number of the men fingered by the Russians could prove that they were not even in the camp when the incident occurred, and their whereabouts were substantiated. That meant that the Russians were lying in a number of instances, and normally the case would have been thrown out of court. But to allow the Russians to save a modicum of face, the men indicted were publicly sentenced to imprisonment and taken off in custody, presumably to detention cells. They were released as soon as the Russians left.

From that point on, American policy changed. Russians were not allowed inside the camp, not even with the American escort which had been provided after the Rhine incident, as much for the Russians' protection as for the DP's. No more Slavs were openly repatriated against their will.

And just to make sure that the Russians wouldn't try anything, the Americans established a special security force made up of men picked from the DP's, issued them carbines and special uniforms, and gave them responsibility for guarding the camp and protecting their own people.

All of which we rejoiced in, because it marked the end of Russian wool being pulled over American eyes, at least in our area, and life gradually settled into a degree of normalcy for us. Father had gotten a job in the local UNRA motor pool, and was now driving a GMC truck for them; Alexei and I were going to trade school, learning to be auto mechanics; and mother—mother was slowly growing better, but still so sick that Belgium wouldn't even consider our application for a visa to go there, nor would Venezuela, where father had applied three times. (There was no point in even applying to America; unless you had relatives there to sponsor you, you didn't have a chance.)

This was a particularly difficult time for father, who was growing increasingly concerned for our immediate safety as well as long-term well-being (for in those days phrases like "Iron Curtain" and "Cold War" were just beginning to come into usage, and no one could really be sure of anything in Europe, especially that the Communists would not have their way in Germany before too long). Therefore, his primary goal in life was to get us as far away from Russia as possible, and since America was out of the question, Venezuela would have to do.

The third time Venezuela turned him down, in the fall of '47, he reached the end of his rope. Weeping bitter tears of frustration, with nowhere else to turn, he did something completely out of character for him: he turned to God (at mother's urging, I suspect, for her own faith seemed to be growing quietly). "All right!" father exclaimed to God," if You'll take us to America, I'll believe in You and give You my life. But only *after* we're all there!" It wasn't much of a turning—it was more of a challenge really, because he knew how impossible it was—but there it was.

We didn't know quite what to make of it, nor, I suppose did father, who promptly forgot about it. He had other things to think about: Ivan Ivanovich Basansky was born on February 26, 1948— "the child of their old age," though Father was all of thirty-five at the time.

In October of 1948, they closed down the DP camp at Mainz-Kestel, and we were transferred to the one at Hanau, of all places. UNRA's central motor pool was located in Offenbach, just a short truck-ride from Hanau, and father got a good job there, driving again. By now Alexei and I were seventeen and sixteen, and both pretty fair apprentice mechanics, so father was able to get us jobs in the service end of the motor pool.

So now we were all making good money, the girls themselves were twelve and thirteen, little Johnny was doing fine (we Americanized his name from the start), and mother was finally coming into health. Our life was more than tolerable; it was pretty good. And we had accepted the probability that we would be staying in Germany, and didn't really mind—except for the fear that was always there. We knew the Communists; we knew how long they remembered, and how patiently they could wait for an opportunity to settle a score. And they were growing stronger and more confident every day. Their blockading of Berlin had been going on for nine months, and it looked as if they were going to win that contest of wills. In short, the fear that just the mention of their name was capable of producing in us was as strong as ever.

This was the nature of our thinking that spring of 1949, when the word came down that America was now opening its doors to war orphans. Immediately, we all thought of

Lydia. It had been five years since her mother had left her with us in Strukyvka, and we had never heard anything of her since. For all intents and purposes, Lydia was an orphan, and here suddenly and unexpectedly was the prize beyond compare: a chance to go to America! The administration office of the camp accepted our application on her behalf, and Lydia was on her way to become part of an American family—at least one of us had made it!

But when, three months later, out of the clear blue, a man from the camp's administration office asked mother if all of us would like to go as a family, she dismissed it as some kind of joke. He had to come back and ask her again, before she realized that he was serious. The opportunity was this: an American lawyer named Rodman in Washington, North Carolina, had a large farm and wanted a whole family to work on it, the larger and the more men, the better. He had formerly had German prisoners-of-war working it, and they had gone home, so now he was willing to sponsor a DP family. The agreement was that we would work for him for one year, to pay back his expenses for bringing us over, after which we were free to go wherever we wanted. Without further hesitation, mother put in an application for us.

Needless to say, it sounded too good to be true, when she told us about it; there had to be something wrong with it, somewhere. "Don't even bother looking for something wrong," father said. "There's just not a chance that it will ever happen. It's ridiculous to even consider it!"

A picture was taken of us and sent to America, along with a detailed report on us, and final approval came back, pending the physical. Well, there it was: the physical—the impossible obstacle that father had referred to without knowing it. Mother would never pass. We had already been turned down on previous applications to other countries because of mother's health.

But it wasn't mother who flunked the physical; it was me. Mother had healed remarkably; either that, or the doctors had had an astonishing lapse of discernment (either way, I could see Babunia smiling). And father was almost completely healed of his paralysis (he *is* healed completely now—the only case I know of, of such a total recovery from wood alcohol poisoning). And there was nothing wrong with Alexei or Lida or Johnny. But Vasili had tubercular spots on his lungs. The X-rays showed them, very clearly.

Well, we had come so close. And after all of us had long since given up hope. There was another possibility that crossed everyone's mind then, so I finally spoke it: "Listen, there's no point in all of us missing what may be the only chance we'll ever get, just because one of us has some spots on his lungs. You go now, and then you can send for me, when you're established. You'll be my relatives in America!" I added, doing my best to make a light thing of it.

But no one said anything; they didn't even manage a weak smile. The silence hung heavy as we waited. Finally, father said, "This family has been through too much as a family, to start operating any differently now. We go together, or we don't go at all. I have said it, and that's that!" he added with a dash of the old autocratic finality that I used to hate so much and now could kiss him for. And I did, with big tears rolling down my cheeks. And then we all hugged one another, and cried. And it didn't matter so much that we weren't going to America.

Except that we were. I was told to come back for another X-ray. Why, or who initiated it, I will never know, except that it wasn't any one of us. And I passed that X-ray with flying colors—not even a trace of a spot.

On August 28, 1949, we embarked from Bremerhaven, and then went up the gangplank of that American transport. I am sure that I was not the only one who felt a tangible difference between the atmosphere on the dock and on the ship. It was like walking out of a gray shroud and coming into the light. You nod, Babunia, I thought, and you smile; you see, I am learning.

Ten days later—ten days of living a dream and not daring to believe that we were living and not dreaming it—we steamed into New York harbor. And slowly on the left, we passed the Statue of Liberty, her torch of freedom raised aloft, and in her pedestal, the famous words:

> *Give me your tired, your poor,*
> *Your huddled masses yearning to breathe free,*
> *The wretched refuse of your teeming shore.*
> *Send these, the homeless, tempest-tossed to me.*
> *I lift my lamp beside the golden door!*

epilogue

There are two more incidents that belong in this book. The first took place on the way to Mr. Rodman's farm. After some harrowing misadventures, which I will not go into here, the foreman had collected us and what little baggage we had and was driving us through the town of Washington, North Carolina, when it occurred to him that we might enjoy some Coke and candy.

He pulled up in front of the local supermarket and got out to get it, and as an afterthought, waved for us to come on inside with him. We hurried to do so, and as we walked past the cash registers (something we had never done in Europe, where you told someone what you wanted, and they got it for you, rather than trust you), I could not believe my eyes! There was food everywhere, endless supplies of it! And not just grain or vegetables either, but beautiful food, too, in bright packages, and whole shelves full of candy! And fresh milk, more than any one person could drink in a

189

month! And eggs in cartons, and a pyramid of oranges, and—when I saw the golden jars with the pictures of bees on them, I stopped in my tracks: I knew instinctively that they were honey. And then I remembered the last thing that Babunia ever said to us: God is going to take you to a Land of Milk and Honey.

The other incident happened several years later. Father received a letter smuggled out of the Ukraine from a Christian, also named Ivan, whom he had known in the Nazi labor camp at Mainz. Father had not been interested in Ivan's faith at that time, but had told him about Babunia's, since Babunia had seemed to feel as strongly about God and Jesus Christ as his friend Ivan did.

Ivan seemed fascinated with Babunia, with her secret faith and the stories she told. Father was not able to tell him that much, however, and dismissed the whole thing from his mind, as one of those interests which take on unusual emphasis in prison. So he was very much surprised to get a letter from Ivan.

The letter said that Ivan had gone back to Strukyvka after the war and had found Babunia—alive. He had told her of all the miracles of divine intervention that father had related to him without recognizing that that was what they were. And Babunia had laughed and said she knew.

And then he had told her of father's determination that, no matter what, they were not going back to the Ukraine, and Babunia had accepted this with great peace and had told her Lord that she was ready to go to be with Him now. And soon after that, she did.

One evening, while my father was away, I asked Babunia why he was the way he was, when she and mother were so different. She looked into the fire and pursed her lips before answering: "In the olden days, they used to say that if a man were bitter and hated enough, an evil spirit would come into him and possess him." Something in my expression must have told Babunia how hard I found that to accept. "Well," she said, with a smile and a shrug, "*kto znaet*—who can say? There's no question he'd had plenty to be bitter about." And that night, we heard the real-life story of Ivan Savielevich Basansky.

Like my mother Maria's family, Ivan's were *Kulaki*, well-to-do farmers. For generations they had had more than a hundred hectares of forest and fields, stables, and servants to see to their every need. The fact that their name ended in y, instead of i, had the same significance as the prefix von before a German name, a sign of aristocracy.

Ivan was barely five, that day in the fall of 1917, when the Bolsheviks pounded on his family's door and informed them that they had one hour to gather their belongings and clear off "the people's property." But their belongings did not include horses or wagons; they too, belonged to "the people." Due to the upheaval that swept the land during harvest time, or perhaps to God's displeasure, there was a crop failure that fall, which was followed by an extremely severe winter. All across the snowbound steppes famine raged, and the thousands of former land owners who had been turned out of their homes had no food, or even work or shelter, for those who still had their homes were afraid to employ them, much less take them in. They made do the best they could, but it was not long before a typhoid epidemic decimated their ranks.

When Ivan's parents, weakened by hunger and the extreme cold, caught the fever and died, such was the fear of

three

It was my father! But it couldn't be! Alexei had said he was up north, in one of the armies defending Kiev. Yet here he came, and Moryak was with him. And though he ran in a crouch, every so often his head would bob above the rim of the gully, and almost immediately spurts of dirt would kick up along the rise behind where his head had just been.

Alexei was watching, too. "Someone over there has a pair of field glasses and is directing that gun's fire!" he shouted. "Now they *must* be convinced that the Germans have arrived!" And sure enough, all along the line, the firing suddenly intensified.

"Alexei! Vasili!" father yelled as he came. "Keep down!" As if we had any intention of doing anything else.

Reaching the three of us, he threw himself against the near side of the gully and struggled for breath. My feelings were in a turmoil: part of me was glad to see him, grateful that he had come for us; the other part dreaded the sight of him. But before I could sort out what I felt, Alexei asked, "Father, what are you doing here?"

Our father looked at him for a moment before answering. "I and a few others were lucky enough to escape from the Uman encirclement. The Germans came from the north, down through Belaya Tserkov and Novo Arkhangelsk; from the west, through Vinnitsa; and from the south, across the Dniester. They closed the circle at Pervomaysk, and I heard they took more than one hundred thousand prisoners."

He stopped for breath, and to see how we were taking what he said. "The Sixth, Twelfth and Eighteenth Armies were smashed," he clapped his hands together and held them out to us, palms up. "They simply do not exist any more. I tried to cross the Dneiper, to be re-assigned, but they've blown all the bridges. And as you can see," he added, gesturing in the direction of the far shore, "they're shooting at anything that moves. So, here I am."

"But father," persisted Alexei, "we heard that Stalin had given the order: 'Stand fast and die.' And if a hundred thousand prisoners *were* taken, how come—"

"Listen!" our father hissed, "We were issued one rifle for every fifty men! And three bullets for each rifle! You think that's going to stop the Panzerkorps?" His eyes narrowed. "Or maybe you'd be happier if I were starving to death in some German prisoner-of-war camp?"

Alexei and I knew it was time to keep silent. After the Duduj, my father was the main source of fear in my life—a real, known source. Such was his temper that, though not that large, he would take on someone twice his size in an instant, if he thought he had been crossed in any way. He feared no man, "not even the devil himself," as Babunia would say. Not even Babunia's husband, though until the latter died of a fever, my father used to sleep with a knife

under his mattress, in case he should ever come after him.

And there was a good chance that that might happen, because my father was also the meanest man I ever knew. Whenever he did come home, he was usually drunk, and he would either beat us up or my mother, when she came home from work. One day, he beat her so badly that she stood bent double, blood flowing from her ears and nose.

I ran outside screaming, trying to get someone to stop him, before he killed her. But those whom I saw either went on as if they hadn't heard me, or they just laughed at me—in the new Russia, contrary to propaganda, the men consider themselves definitely superior beings. Women are there primarily to satisfy them, and any man who doesn't beat his wife from time to time is less than a man. My father was even more manly; he beat Babunia too, but only after her husband was safely in the ground.

The most frightening thing about my father's rages was that he beat us for no discernible reason. If you spoke to him, he'd beat you for that; if you didn't, he'd beat you for that. If you moved while he was hitting you, he'd beat you the harder. And if you didn't move, that so incensed him that he was likely to tie you to a post and whip you like an animal, with one of the bullwhips he liked to make. When he did that, you couldn't take your shirt off afterwards, because it would be stuck in the grooves in your skin.

It was even worse, if that was possible, when you did give him a reason. One spring, Alexei and I had gone down to the Dnieper and were throwing stones in the water. Alexei got his *valenki* wet—his new, heavy felt boots that father had just bought for him. When father learned of it, he screamed and grabbed Alexei, hoisting him over his head like a sack of potatoes and flinging him on the ground—so hard that Alexei's lungs were torn loose from his rib cage, and he very nearly died.

relatives and former friends that no one would risk taking
Ivan, his three-year-old sister Fenka, and their six-month-
old baby brother Victor. And so they were shipped off to
one of the new orphanages run by the government. Or
rather, *not* run would be more accurate, for there was no
heat except in the staff's quarters, very little food, and
supervision consisted of them beating you as readily as
looking at you. And there were more mouths to feed every
day, for the Revolution had produced one bumper crop:
orphans.

Little Victor soon died of malnutrition. Somehow Ivan
and Fenka survived for five years—five years that would fill
any person's stomach with hate, Babunia said. Finally Ivan
escaped at the age of ten, becoming a *khuligan*, an outlaw,
living by his wits in the streets. There, his instinct for survival was honed, and his hardening completed. He would
think nothing of hitting a man over the head and taking
whatever he happened to need at the time. Which was
usually food, for famine stalked the city streets even more
than the country roads. On two occasions he was enticed
into, and barely escaped from, homes where they would
lure people in and butcher them, dressing the meat and
selling it in the marketplace at exorbitant prices.

Of course, in the new Russia, there were not supposed to
be any khuligans, so officially my father did not exist. But
the truth was, he was learning quite a bit about the business
of existing, and this knowledge, coupled with an indomitable will to survive, was now capable of taking him coolly to
the very brink of hell and back—and indeed had, not once
but several times, by the time he met my mother.

"In fact, his will to live is almost more than human,"
Babunia said, concluding her story and pausing to look at
me. "Like yours, the way you fought to get out of that snake
pit." (I had told her of the dream I'd had, that day I went

through the ice). "Whatever it is that drives your father, Vasya, I suspect it drives you, too. I wonder what else that will of yours is going to get you out of—or into." She gazed into the fire. "I wonder how long it will take you to reach the light at the top of the hill." And we both tried to see the future through the flames.

"Tracers!" my father exclaimed. And in the twilight, what looked like streams of shooting stars began to pass overhead. Alexei, seeing the puzzled look on my face and anxious to show off in front of father, took pity on his uninformed subordinate and explained: "In the machine-gun belts, at night every fifth round is an incendiary. This enables the gunner to actually see where his fire is going and lay it accordingly."

Father seemed not to hear, concentrating instead on the rapidly-darkening sky to the west. "A few minutes more, and they won't be able to make out silhouettes. We can go home then, and drop this fellow off at his house," and he tousled Georgi's hair, acknowledging his existence for the first time. "I imagine his parents are a little concerned," he said, laughing—it was hard to tell whether in sympathy or scorn. That was the thing about my father: you never could be sure what was going on inside of him. Nor could you say that he was all bad. But that didn't stop me from hating him—so much that I had promised myself that one day I would kill him. I imagined it with a gun, up close so that I could watch his face as the bullets went in.

And yet, he had come back for us.

The stars were beginning to come out, and looking up at them for some reason I thought of another starry night, a few weeks earlier. On that occasion I was waiting with my mother, instead of my father—crouched down as here, but not moving a muscle. We were in the cornfield of another collective farm, and we were about to indulge in some "borrowing." But first we had to ascertain the whereabouts of the watchman[1] and wait until he was safely distant.

We were fortunate that night; there was no moon. In the vast darkness, even with our eyes fully adjusted to the faint starlight, we would have to move more by feel than by sight. I looked up at the stars—so many, so peaceful, so close somehow—and wondered. And made a note to ask Babunia about them.

Just then, my mother tapped my arm twice. Moving slowly enough that a mistake would not be heard, and taking care to breathe through our mouths, we began to pick ears of corn. After what seemed like half the night, we had filled a gunny sack, and eased out of the field, into the cover of some nearby trees.

Suddenly a twig snapped, off to our left. At that instant, everything in me wanted to cry out, but such was my training that, like my mother, I merely froze. The fear produced needle-like pain in my body. When mother decided it was safe, we moved on. Several kilometers away, we stuffed the sack with straw and buried it deep enough so that with the straw it would not freeze. Marking the location with a

---

[1]To keep the underfed people of the village from stealing "the people's food," the Communists set watchmen in every large field, day and night. The penalties for being caught were severe: if a worker so much as grabbed a head of wheat in his fist, shucked off the grains, and licked them into his mouth, it could cost him half a day's labor points. Two weeks before our nocturnal foray, a man my mother knew had been sentenced to three years in prison for taking one ear of corn.

But the penalty for *not* stealing was even more severe: almost certain starvation.

couple of fair-sized rocks, we left, and would avoid coming anywhere near that place again—until another night, just before the ground froze solid, when we would have real need of those ears of corn.

When we finally reached the safety of the house, I asked mother why our precautions had had to be so elaborate. She was a little put out, as if the answer were obvious. "Vasili, you may be quite old for your age; hunger does that, and having to do what we have to, to stay alive. But you still have much to learn about people: the reward for turning in a food-thief is food." And she stopped there, as if that explained it.[2]

---

[2]By this time the Communists' instrument of subjection-by-starvation was finely tuned. *Too* many deaths, they had found, eventually affected the efficiency of the food-producing collective units; they knew just how far they could turn the screws of hunger before people became too weak to work, or in such despair that they might do something foolish. Indeed, so precise was this "science," that for each laying hen that a family owned, the government required that family to turn in 300 eggs a year. As anyone who has had anything to do with chickens knows, occasionally you do find a hen that can manage six eggs a week, but five is more normal, and that can drop to four or even three in the summer.

More often than not, the family would wind up short of its quota, but the quota still had to be met, and the government didn't care how; one could always trade other produce to acquire the extra eggs, and the government suspected that there were chickens that had been hidden from the scrutiny of their inspectors. The main thing was that most families who owned any livestock—cows or pigs or chickens—found themselves perpetually in debt to the government, which was exactly the way the government wanted it.

But such precision—so many eggs per hen per year, so many liters of milk per cow (for every ten liters you turned in, they gave

I asked Babunia about it, the next morning, as Alexei and I helped her in the garden, and she pointed out that every square centimeter of ground that surrounded our house was under cultivation. (And Babunia could grow an onion in the dirt you could hold in one hand.) Even the pots that sat on the window sills in the house could be counted on for a few onions each. She reminded me also of the keep-hole, in which we stored everything that we didn't need and that would keep, and that when we caught a fish, we boiled the heads and the scales and ate the gel that was made of their residue—every possible bit of nourishment was precious. In fact, our entire summer was spent earning, growing, catching and "borrowing" enough food to see us through the winter. Even then, there would be many cold days with nothing but herb-and-potato soup, if that. And if God did not provide—through fish or windfall or miracle—Babunia had said, we would not make it. But God had provided.

Recalling her words, I looked up at the night sky. There, beyond the streams of tracers, were the stars, just as before.

-----

you back two, after first removing the fat), sixty per cent of each pig (the *best* sixty per cent, and you had to have their permission to slaughter)—was not arrived at easily. Many "mistakes" were made in the early years, and occasionally the instrument was overtuned: in the winter of 1932, the year I was born, the famine was so widespread that people started eating their domestic animals. And when all the dogs and cats were gone, some started eating their children, beginning with the youngest, while nearby, the Communists stood guard over storehouses full of grain.

A mistake? Perhaps. In any event, it served to accomplish the same end: the breaking of the Ukrainian will to resist. How many were exterminated over the years in this fashion? The printed estimates that I have seen are in the fifteen million range, and I believe them to be conservative.

"Come on, dreamer, we're moving!" my father barked at me, and without even a glance to see if we were following him, he headed up the gully on the run, crouched over as he had come. The three of us clambered along after him, as quickly as we could, and Moryak brought up the rear.

When we reached the village, it all seemed like a strange dream. Instead of being totally dark, the houses were silhouetted against a dull, red glow, as several of the thatched roofs had been set afire by the tracers. Every so often, there would be a flash and a *crump,* and a geyser of dirt would go up in the road, or the side of a house would collapse. As my eyes grew accustomed to the scene, I saw that families were huddled behind their houses, on the side farthest from the shooting. I was about to ask father why, when Alexei beat me to it. Because, father told us, the machine-gun bullets would go through one wall but would be too spent to get through the second.

Surprisingly, moving was not that difficult. Listening carefully and watching for muzzle flashes in the dark, we knew when to run and when to sit tight behind a building. We made it to our house without too much trouble, and there, all wrapped in blankets and sitting on the ground with their backs to the wall, were Babunia and mother and Lida. They were as glad to see us, as we them, and Moryak was the happiest of all. We frolicked in the little safe space behind the house, while father took Georgi home.

I snuggled down next to Babunia, and despite the noise and bursts of light from the exploding shells, I began to feel drowsy and noted that Alexei and Lida and mother were already asleep. But tonight was too important a night to waste on sleeping! I wondered what it would be like when the Germans came. Would they treat us like the Communists had? Or set us free to live our own lives? The feeling I got from Alexei and from the grown-ups was that, even if they treated us as captives, nothing could be as bad as it was before. It was almost certain that mother would not have to work sixteen hours a day to earn enough labor-points.

The thought of labor-points made me think of what had happened just the week before. During the last three weeks of harvest, which was even then being completed, the work was harder than at any other time of the year, and Alexei and I had gone into the fields to help mother finish her assignment. It was sickle-and-scythe work—slow, back-breaking, exhausting—cutting the wheat by hand and gathering it into sheaves, to be picked up by the wagon. Mother did that, and then she loaded the sheaves onto the wagon and unloaded them at the thresher—as many as 3,500 sheaves herself in one day.

The thresher would separate the grain of wheat from the chaff, and the leftover straw would be piled on pallets and drawn up on top of either of two huge towers of straw, by horses pulling on cables. These two straw towers would be three or four houses high, and would provide fodder for all the collective's farm animals through the winter. On the flat steppes, they could be seen for thirty kilometers, far above any other structure, like the domes of the old churches in the larger towns.

At the end of the afternoon, when we were so tired we could hardly move, mother would send us home to supper, and Babunia would rub our arms with an ointment that she had made. Then, after supper we would sit on the front step and wait for sunset. First to come home were the cows. A few of them had bells, and these could be heard well before they actually came into view. One of the old men of the village acted as cowherd for those who owned cows, taking his charges out in the morning, finding them pasture-land, and leading them home, as they followed him down the road, lowing to those that waited for them with hay and fresh water. When each cow came to its own home, it simply turned in at the gate and went straight to its stall, to eat and drink and be milked. And the cowherd walked on through the village until the last cow was safely delivered. Even as a boy, I thought this was one of the most beautiful things I had ever seen—these cows turning in one by one at their respective houses.

About the time the milking was done, and the shadows of dusk were gathering into night, you could hear the workers coming home from the fields. Having stopped at a gathering place to pick up their belongings, they would be coming home in a group. And they would be singing the ballads of old Russia, that their fathers and grandfathers, and *their* fathers had sung before them.

They sang, not out of joy, but out of exhaustion, so tired that singing was the only thing that could revive them.[3] And

---

[3] Exhaustion was the third great enemy, after hunger and fear, and all three were continually with us. The hunger was such that, even on the rare occasion of a full meal, when you had eaten so much that you could scarcely breathe, your stomach was still suspicious: how long would it be till the next time it was full?

The fear was like an invisible poisonous gas. It so permeated the very fabric of your life that it seemed to have a stench and taste and color all its own. Years after you had come to freedom, it could ice your heart in an instant. A knock at the door could raise you straight up in bed. Was it the *chornaya vorona*, the black crow of the KGB?

Westerners visiting Russia can't understand why the Russians seem to speak in whispers, as though they were telling secrets; it comes from never being sure who might be listening (like inmates in a prison compound). Westerners also find it hard to understand why the Ukrainians and others didn't revolt. The answer is equally simple: a conspiracy requires more than one, when you since singing was the one place where they could safely express how they really felt, they poured their hearts out in song—and their songs came to embody all the anguish of the motherland, in the greatest travail she had ever known.

In the stillness of the night, you could hear the music in the air, almost before you recognized that that was what it was. It would surge like the sea and swell with power and depth and die away and soar again. And it tore at your heart, till you felt like crying, and you sensed that many who were singing were crying even as they sang. And part of you wished that it would stop because it hurt too much, and yet you knew that it was the most real thing that there was in life.

Even the happy songs, the ones of cows and snowflakes, were edged with sadness, for you knew that the moment the grin disappeared, the ache would return. The singing grew stronger, as the workers approached the village, till it seemed to fill every house, and now you could see the silhouettes, each one turning in at his own gate.

---

cannot trust even the members of your own family, there is no one with whom you dare conspire.

Exhaustion, too, was finely tuned by the Communists. But like "borrowing" corn, or not digging quite as deep for the potatoes at harvest time as one might some night later on, there were ways. A tractor would sheer off the pin of a universal joint, a bolt would somehow fall among the one set of gears in the thresher for which there were no replacement parts on hand. And when the machinery broke down, there was nothing to do but send the workers home early. This gave the workers a chance to tend their home gardens or to sleep.

In the meantime, there were two temporary restoratives: vodka and singing. But vodka cost money and ruined a man for the next day.

Babunia nudged me and pointed to the straw towers at the north end of the village. Tracer bullets had ignited them, and they had become twin spires of flames, reaching to the dark heavens and lighting up the entire village.

four

The next morning, it was as if nothing had happened. The sky stretched clear and deep blue to the golden horizon. And there was silence. The shooting had stopped. Perhaps they realized the Germans weren't there yet and were saving ammunition; possibly they had already withdrawn further. That fall, in full retreat, the Red Army fell back as many as a hundred kilometers in a single day. In any event, except for a few collapsed houses, and craters and pockmarks everywhere, and two columns of smoke rising straight in the still air from the smoldering remains of the straw towers, it was as peaceful as it had been the morning before. The morning before—was it possible that only one day had passed?

"All right, time to wake up! You think all you have to do, now that the Russians are gone, is lie around and sleep?" It was my father speaking, and it was obvious that he had been up for hours, reconnoitering. More likely, he had never gone to sleep.

"Maria, the roof on the granary is partly blown off. Take Vasili and every sack you can find. Nobody knows about it yet, but it won't be long before they all will. We'll have more than twenty kilos of flour this winter, eh?" And he cursed the departed Communists and laughed. "Alexei, you come with me. There's logs floating down Dnieper from where they blew up the floodgates. Some of them are going to our new house." He turned to mother. "How would you like to have a new home, with *four* rooms, eh?" and he gave her a rough hug, the only affection I had ever seen him show towards her.

"Don't waste any time," was his parting comment. "There's no telling when the Germans will get here, or how hard they're going to be. But it will take them a few days to get the lay of the land here, and a lot can be done in the meantime."

Off we went with great excitement. Moryak decided to come with me and mother, who was the happiest I'd seen her in months, getting used to the idea of a new house, and making plans. What a change in her from two weeks before! I thought back to the afternoon she had come home early, because it had been her day to pick up her annual labor-points and the food that they would purchase. It had been obvious that she had been crying. She put a small bag of flour on the table, and when I asked her where the rest was, she started crying again. She told us what had happened. "How do you expect me to feed five people for a year on twenty kilos of flour?" she'd asked them. "That won't last a month!"

"I'm sorry," the man behind the desk had said, smiling and shrugging, "the Party has greater need this year than ever before. This is your share, according to the points you've earned."

"But I worked from four in the morning to nearly ten at night! And I didn't miss a single day, not even when I was sick!"

The man smiled again. "What can I do?"

"If my husband were home, instead of in the front lines, defending the likes of you and your friends, we'd have more points. But he would rather fight than be one of your paid informers, or bribe his way out of going."

The man stopped smiling. "That is beginning to sound counter-revolutionary, comrade," he said icily. "You had better take your flour and go."

There was nothing to do but comply. If she said one more thing, he might very well arrest her under Article 58.[1] And then there would be no one to feed Babunia, the boys and little Lida. She said nothing further, to them or to us. But that night she wrote Ivan a letter—one of the few she had ever written him—telling him of the whole situation. And ten days later he was home.

He never did go any further into the details of his return, nor dared we inquire. However, it was becoming widely known that Russians, who "allowed themselves to be taken prisoner" were being executed as soon as they could be repatriated,[2] in fact, it was a crime to be encircled. Suffice it

---

1. This was the catch-all article in the new government's Criminal Code. It was designed specifically to deal with "counter-revolutionary" activity, and it had fourteen sections, which broadly interpreted, made it quite literally a *catch-all*. For not only were counter-revolutionary words and deeds indictable, but the mere thought—and hence, the suspicion of the thought—was enough for a three-year tour in Siberia. And if the indictment was protested, that was further proof of your anti-Party attitude, and the three years often became seven or even ten.

2. Article 58, section 1, sub-section b, "for action injurious to Soviet military might."

to say that Ivan Basansky was both a natural and con-
ditioned survivor; where hundreds of thousands perished,
he would come through. And mother must have instinctively known this, which explained the letter. Anyway, he
was home now, and as much as I hated him, it felt right to
have him in charge.

When we had successfully carried out our scavenging
assignments, Alexei and I, momentarily with nothing to do,
were fighting as usual. And as usual, Moryak was referee-
ing. He had an uncanny sense of when we were just horsing
around, and when we were really intent on hurting one
another. Whenever it got to be the latter, he himself would
get angry, and come between us growling, keeping us apart
until we calmed down.

All of a sudden, we heard the sound of a motor in the
distance, but it was unlike any we had heard. It wasn't a
truck or a tank, with which we'd grown acquainted when the
Red Army passed through briefly, a few days before. Whatever it was, it was coming from the northwest, and that
could mean only one thing.

"The Germans are coming!" The cry was picked up and
repeated, and it seemed like all of us ran to the center of the
village, to get our first glimpse of our liberators. For by this
time, that's the way everyone was thinking of them—as
liberators. For that matter, I had gathered some ripe apricots that morning, and had them in my hat, as a gift.

With a roar, a motorcycle and sidecar burst into the
village. The motorcycle was driven by a man in a gray
overcoat, helmet, and steel-rimmed goggles, with a sub-
machine gun slung across his back. And in the sidecar, a
surprisingly young man held his high-peaked officer's cap
in his lap and had a shy grin on his face. We all grinned back
and stared at them. I had never seen a motorcycle before,
and my eyes must have been nearly as wide as the driver's
goggles.

"Gray uniforms, not black," Alexei whispered, "that means we're in luck: they're *Wehrmacht*—regular army, not SS."

I had no idea what he was talking about, but it brought me back to earth. Remembering the apricots rolled up in my hat, I hesitantly approached and held them out to the officer. Others began to do the same, offering flowers and fruit and even a chicken, until the crowd of well-wishers around the motorcycle was so thick that it couldn't move.

There was more happiness in the village that day than I had ever known in my life. And it continued that way for six months. The Germans were very relaxed in their occupation. There were not that many of them, and they left us to do pretty much as we pleased. For instance, they let father build his house, without official or administrative permits, and they didn't even ask him why he wasn't working in the fields with the others, or how he happened to be home instead of in the army, since he obviously wasn't wounded or otherwise incapacitated. And they let the other villagers come and help, as many as were able, as was our custom when anyone was building a house. In fact, a few of them, watching the festivities on the perimeter—for afterwards there was a big meal, and someone would bring out an accordion, and there would be singing and even dancing—looked like they were hoping to be asked to join in.

And they never just *took*, but would pay or trade for anything they needed. Thus we were introduced to that marvelous invention, soap. To be sure, they commandeered our harvest, which was now being shipped west instead of east, but they left far more to be divided among the people then the Communists ever had. As a result, for the first time in twenty-four years, we went into winter with enough food on hand to come out the other end.

The day after their arrival, in my initial euphoria I asked Babunia, "Why don't all the Ukrainians in the Red Army

quit and come over to the Germans? Alexei says that Kra
nov, the leader of the Don Cossacks who fought against th
Bolsheviks in 1917, is in Zaporozhye right now, raising nev
regiments of Cossacks to fight alongside the Germans. . . ."

"Sometimes you listen too much to Alexei!" she cut me
off. "The Nazis are no better than the Communists. From
what I hear of Hitler, he's as bad as Stalin, and in my
prayers, God tells me that at the heart, their motivation is as
dark as the Communists'! You see them now as knights and
princes, but wait: the time will come when you will see that
there is not a choice between them. Seeming good cannot
very long come out of evil."

I decided that Babunia was in one of her gloomy spells,
which Alexei confirmed, as soon as I'd told him what she'd
said. But I did not have to wait six months to find out that
she had been right; in fact, I did not have to wait another
day. That afternoon, as Alexei and I and Moryak were
coming from the schoolhouse, we passed by the German
observation post overlooking the Dnieper, just north of the
village. As we ran through the field, Moryak was just ahead
of us. All at once, a shot rang out, and Moryak jerked into
the air and fell on his side. I started to go to him, but Alexei
grabbed my arm. "Target practice!" he hissed. "If they can
do that, they might just as easily shoot us, too!"

Moryak cried out and raised his head to look at us, but we
just stood there, tears streaming down our faces. He held
his head up as long as he could, then blood started running
from his nose, and he whimpered and gnawed at the
ground. I tried to break Alexei's grip and go to him, but he
held fast, and at last Moryak shuddered and lay still.

We ran home, and I threw myself in Babunia's arms and
sobbed my heart out. As I did, she put her hand over my
eyes and spoke to God. My sobs quieted after that, but
whenever I thought of Moryak—that he would never again
play with us, or wake me up when he thought it was time to

get up, or roughhouse with us in the snow—there would be such an emptiness in my heart that I was certain nothing could ever fill it.

The next morning I hated the Germans as much as I had ever hated the Communists. But it would be more than a year before others in our village felt as strongly as I did.

By November, the war had ceased to go well for the Germans. With three million men in more than a hundred divisions, fully a quarter of which were armored *Panzerkorps,* and with unchallenged supremacy in the skies, they had stormed across Byelorussia and the Ukraine like a black typhoon (which, as it happened, was their code name for their offensive against Moscow). Their victories were cataclysmic, unparalleled in the annals of modern warfare— one hundred thousand prisoners taken at Uman, six hundred thousand at Kiev, six hundred and fifty thousand between Bryansk and Vyazma. They had driven all the way to the Don in the south and had laid seige to Leningrad in the north. But in the last two months of 1941, again and again they had been thrown back at the very gates of Moscow in the center. There, for the first time since they had roared into Poland more than two years before and after rolling across all of Europe and most of North Africa, they were forced to go over to the defensive. The myth of German invincibility was broken.[3]

As bad news trickled back to our village from the front— of a Russian counter-offensive all along the thousand-mile

3. The Russians were now joined by the same ally that had enabled them to defeat Napoleon, 130 years before: winter. The Germans, still in their summer uniforms, found that the lubricant in their machine-guns froze at twenty degrees below zero, and their motor oil grew so viscous that they had to light fires under

line from the Baltic to the Black Sea, of von Rundstedt being sacked because he advised pulling back from the Don, of strongpoints having to be supplied by air because the Russians had swept a hundred kilometers past them—the attitude of the Germans toward us began to change. No longer were they so scrupulous about being fair in paying for what they needed; now they offered us receipts redeemable when "the Third Reich's inevitable victory" was accomplished. And though they still left us pretty much alone, the sham of their being our benefactors was wearing thin.

Twice each year, at the end of October and the end of March, the roads in Russia became quagmires of mud, as the fall rains and spring thaw brought to a halt all mechanized warfare for at least three weeks. This abruptly ended the Russian offensive and left both sides exhausted and gasping for breath.

In the Spring of 1942, the Germans were the first to recover. Parrying a weak Soviet thrust at Kharkov, their summer offensive was in full gear by the last week in May. Content to hold their winter lines in the north and center, they gambled everything on a thrust to the south, towards both the precious oil fields of the Caucasus, and the prize of Stalingrad, commanding the Volga.

Despite a disastrous winter campaign and serious shortages of men and equipment, the Germans were still the masters of *blitzkrieg*—lightning war. By July 3, the fortress of Sevastopol fell to them after holding out for 254 days, and with it went the whole Crimea. On August 23, the

---

their tanks to get them started. By February 28, they themselves had lost in excess of one million men, roughly a third of their entire eastern fighting force. Of these, frostbite alone had claimed more than a hundred thousand. Now it was Hitler who gave the order to "Stand fast and die."

German Sixth Army reached the Volga, just above Stalin-grad, and two days later the First Panzer Army had taken Maikop and was within eighty kilometers of the main Soviet oil center at Grozny, and barely 150 kilometers from the Caspian Sea. Once again, the German eagle seemed to stand astride the world.

In our village, the renewed optimism of our "liberators" was making itself felt. Though they were under explicit orders to ship out our entire harvest to the Fatherland, some of these young Germans were farmboys themselves, and they did not post guards over the fields at night. So once again we entered winter in better shape than we had since the Revolution.

But that winter proved to be the worst for the Germans in at least that long. No longer were the tanks slashing down the summer roads and wheeling out across the steppes in classic battle formation. What tanks were left lacked the fuel for extended maneuvers. Now it was a different kind of war, a war of ghosts in white parkas, gliding across the top of the snow, disappearing and re-appearing in totally un-expected locations—Russian ghosts. It had become a stationary war, a war of waiting in fox-holes in snow that looked exactly the same everywhere, a war of trying to see the enemy before it was too late, of cold that stung and quickly numbed like a syringe full of novocaine, of gnawing on numbed frozen rations, when there was anything to eat at all. A war of lonely, pitiful death.

Though the Germans had committed all their reserves to the effort, they failed to take Stalingrad. And because they *had* thrown everything into that last, desperate lunge, their flank along the Don was dangerously exposed and de-fended only by three light-infantry divisions—poorly equipped Romanians, Italians, and Hungarians. These fought gallantly, but were soon cut to pieces by a massive onslaught of fresh Soviet armor, and in a thunderclap the